UNVEILING YOUR VIRTUE

*How to Find Your Self-Value
and Worth through Christ*

Melissa Ann DeSerio

BALBOA.PRESS

A DIVISION OF HAY HOUSE

This book is a work of non-fiction. Unless otherwise noted, the author and the publisher make no explicit guarantees as to the accuracy of the information contained in this book and in some cases, names of people and places have been altered to protect their privacy.

Scripture quotations marked KJV are from the Holy Bible, King James Version (Authorized Version). First published in 1611. Quoted from the KJV Classic Reference Bible, Copyright © 1983 by The Zondervan Corporation.

Balboa Press books may be ordered through booksellers or by contacting:

Balboa Press
A Division of Hay House
1663 Liberty Drive
Bloomington, IN 47403
www.balboapress.com
844-682-1282

Because of the dynamic nature of the Internet, any web addresses or links contained in this book may have changed since publication and may no longer be valid. The views expressed in this work are solely those of the author and do not necessarily reflect the views of the publisher, and the publisher hereby disclaims any responsibility for them.

The author of this book does not dispense medical advice or prescribe the use of any technique as a form of treatment for physical, emotional, or medical problems without the advice of a physician, either directly or indirectly. The intent of the author is only to offer information of a general nature to help you in your quest for emotional and spiritual well-being. In the event you use any of the information in this book for yourself, which is your constitutional right, the author and the publisher assume no responsibility for your actions.

Cover image by Kourtney Leech

Print information available on the last page.

ISBN: 978-1-9822-7808-3 (sc)
ISBN: 978-1-9822-7810-6 (hc)
ISBN: 978-1-9822-7809-0 (e)

Library of Congress Control Number: 2021924879

Balboa Press rev. date: 12/10/2021

Unveiling Your Virtue:
How to Find Your Self-Value and Worth through Christ

Melissa Ann DeSerio
Founder and President of Joy Today Ministries, Inc.

To my late husband, John Michael DeSerio.

My three sons, Landen, Hunter, and Hayden. My loves.

And special thanks to my encourager and
spiritual mom. Carol Valentino.

Contents

Foreword

The word "virtue" is used to describe the quality of a person's character. *The Oxford Dictionary* defines it as the equality of being good or excellent; excellence in one's own right, especially by doing what is right and being kind to others.

Melissa has been evangelizing, teaching, and mentoring young and elderly brethren for over twenty years now, and I am excited to write this foreword for her first book.

She is an amazing woman who has helped me become more confident in my ability to be a better me. Some writers have nonpersonal experiences with a story's subject but she is different.

Through the Holy Spirit, she will guide you in how to achieve success by virtue, show you how to live your life according to your values and principles, help you find your purpose—as I have found mine—teach you how to live your life based on what makes you happy, and show you how to live your life based on what makes you feel good about yourself.

Stay blessed.

Donald Umeh

Introduction

Holy Spirit, you are the Creator.

Holy Spirit, you are the action of God.

Holy Spirit, you take what is invisible, and your make the visible out of it.

And the Holy Spirit is here to do nothing except what it is commanded from heaven.

The Holy Spirit can only do what the Father says to do!

You get a flavor of that in Joshua, when he's talking to the angel of the Lord, and the angel of the Lord says, "I'm not for you and I'm not for them I serve the Lord." So the angel of the Lord only takes orders from the Father.

And that is exactly how it works with the Holy Spirit on earth. He only takes orders from the Father. If the Father does not speak, he—the Holy Spirit—does not have anything to do. He operates out of the mind of Christ which is the will of the Father on earth.

"So let this mind be in you ... that was in Christ." This is a manifestation of the sons of God.

Let's Define the Purpose of this Book

The purpose of this book is challenge you, friend, to search your heart and truly begin to enter into an intimate relationship with your heavenly father and discover who you really are. To never again undervalue your worth and divine purpose on this earth. For as he is, so are you and I in this world. First John 4:17 (KJV) tells us, Herein is our love made perfect, that we may have boldness the day of judgement: because as he is, so are we in this world.

To realize the importance of abiding "in" Christ Jesus, John 15:4 (KJV) says, Abide in me, and I in you. As the branch cannon bear fruit of itself, except it abide in the vine, neither can you unless you remain in me"; to make sure you understand the importance and value of a true divine friend; to add value to your life; and to equip and encourage you to be the best you, you can be. And perhaps most important, to understand your worth and that completeness is not in another human being or materialistic things. It's only found as you abide in him, Christ Jesus, in a divine intimate relationship with your heavenly Father in whom I marvel at referring to as my daddy, my best friend, my Savior, Abba Father, El Shaddal, the God who is more than enough.

God sees every tear you have cried, and has felt every tormenting pain you have endured but on a much deeper level. I want you to walk away from this book transformed, equipped, encouraged, and on a higher level in your life. Knowing more of your value, more of your exact blueprint, realizing once and for all that you do matter and have real, shiny gold in you. Real worth; your existence matters.

That you realize you truly have a gigantic purpose for existing. Yes, you. You have a divine purpose in this life on this planet. Your existence truly matters, dear friend. And I say those words with great pride and grace. I scream grace to your mountain. I say, "Come, Holy Spirit, come Holy Spirit, come Holy Spirit. Flood this book, flood the atmosphere and minds of those reading this. Consume them with the one and only precious and beautiful Holy Spirit. Create in them a boldness and yearning like never before to want to sit down and truly read their Bible and pray."

The question of the hour is this: Will you truly let Jesus into your heart? Or will you continue looking for a person or material thing to fill the void that truly only be filled by a divine relationship while abiding in him, your one and only true Savior, Jesus Christ. He is the God who satisfies with a long life and who came so that you and I might not just live but live abundantly. This love cannot be acquired by any other way than truly accepting Jesus into your heart and abiding in him.

Can you feel and see that there is gold in you? Do you truly grasp that you have real gold in you? From the moment you were conceived in your mother's womb, you had value, deep value. When I say you have gold in you, I use "gold" as a metaphor symbolizing the depth and weight and dunamis that only comes from developing a one-on-one relationship with your heavenly Father, Savior, best friend, Abba Father, precious, and beautiful Holy Spirit, lover of my soul, Jesus Christ.

So I'm walking in the church, and a gentlemen walks up to me and says, "You know what, Miss? God sent me to tell you there is gold in you." When I asked what he meant, he replied, "I see the gold in you. You are precious to the Lord."

Forget the past; forget all your past mistakes. Never mind what anyone has said or is saying. I see the gold in you. From that moment on, I never looked at myself or my circumstances the same. The man said, "You deserve to be happy. You deserve to have a good life." When he asked if he could please pray for me, of course I said yes. He pulled a chair over to the altar and told me to sit down. He laid his hands on me and prayed with everything in him. I felt the glory of God come all over me and received healing. At that moment the Lord spoke to me and told me something very special was about to happen.

The purpose of this book is to help you realize there is gold in every single one of us. It doesn't matter who you are, what you have, where you live, or what you've been through. Friend, there is gold in you. From the moment you were conceived in your mother's womb, there was gold in you. God is patiently waiting for you to step out of that uncertainty and lack and say, "I choose to be everything my heavenly Father created me to be."

Search yourself. Are you hanging with people who celebrate you? Or are you hanging where you are tolerated? It's time to do a reality check. Don't let people make you settle for less than Papa has for you. If you're not at peace within yourself, you're not where you should be. Jesus came to give you life, to give you life abundantly. I want you to ask yourself the following questions. Write the answers down on paper and pray over them.

Are you growing in your Christian walk?
Are you reading your Bible enough?
Are you praying enough?
Are you taking the time to stop and truly smell the roses?

Don't let people's jealousies and insecurities hold you back from being everything you see God calling you to be. Dare to dream. Let go of the past. Let go of that horrible relationship you once had. Let go of the old you. Realize that God has an even better relationship and new life waiting for you if you will but step into it. Go on that trip you've dreamed of. Meet up with that special somebody. Dance again; laugh again. Allow yourself to live again! What does living again mean to you? Perhaps to live again means to commute and truly fellowship with who, friend? Are you fellowshipping with the Father? Do you spend time with him in the quiet place daily?

Ask yourself this one question: If you were to die this very second, where would you go? Do you know without a shadow of a doubt where you would go? If you find yourself overthinking about it, get on your knees, go to God, and ask him to change your thinking.

Enough of the reaching out to people who don't respond or truly do not care. Let them go. Pray, ask God to bring you divine relationships that will help you flourish. Dream big. See yourself with the spouse of your dreams, living in the house of your dreams. Life doesn't stop for anyone. Sure, things happen that make us feel like giving up. Learn to put your emotions aside, and stop the stinking thinking.

Choose to be single-minded. No more double-mindedness. For as he is, so are you and I in this world. The key here is to remember we are to model our lives after our Savior, Jesus Christ. Jesus's words are meaningful and bold. He never wallowed in self-pity or be overwhelmed. He was slow to speak and quick to listen. He said what needed to be said, shrugged it off, and moved on. So friends, don't waste your valuable time worrying about people who will not even return your phone call or text. Move on, pray, ask God to send you the right people who have been assigned to your life. Let there be balance in your life. Illuminate the majestic things in your life that God has graciously given you. Grace be unto you! Don't pass up the blessings God is trying to give you.

Release the toxic thoughts, and replace them with God's Word. Better than that, find some people to bless. When God gives you that special person you've prayed for, marvel every second you have with that person. Take hold of the blessing and honor it. Truly allow the Lord to replace your ashes with beauty. We all go thought seasons; don't stay in that season. Jump out of it with joy and allow yourself to love again. As my ninety-seven-year-old grandmother told me, "God is love."

Everything in life revolves around, in, and through love. God is pure agape love. You see, when you do not trust the Lord, you are being double-minded. And we are to remain single-minded like our Savior, Jesus Christ. Don't let the enemy steal your blessings. Life is about the moments that take your breath away. So stop, smell those roses, and lend a hand to that neighbor and friend. True character is helping others who cannot help you in return. It's not expecting anything in return. Rise up, rise up out of that bed and stand. Stand tall for Jesus, and he will stand tall for you. He will even carry you. He will never leave or forsake you. Call him on his word. Watch him bless you. Simply bow before him, and surrender all unto him.

As a little girl I remember wanting nothing more than to spend quality time with my mother. I prayed day and night, believing God would bring it to pass. Well guess what happened when I was fifteen. We were reunited. It was so hard to find out she was in a mental institution, behind bars with very depressed people who were screaming and battling so many demons.

I didn't understand why this happened to her? Why was she left here? My heart hurt so badly for her. I wondered, *How could anybody just leave such a beautiful woman in this horrible place?* As I approached the door to see her, I prayed really hard, "Father, please do not let any of these screaming people be my mother." Sure enough, out came this beautiful, blonde, gentle woman with a white crocheted sweater. She was not screaming; she was scared. She approached me with a gentle hug. I held back the tears and quickly gathered her up with her overnight bag and took her with me for the weekend.

As we approached each other for the first time in fourteen years, there was such a joy, a pure joy that could only come from heaven. That special joy when you see your parent whom you love so dearly. As a child I was told all kinds of crazy things about her. "Your mother is nuts. Let her go. She is schizophrenic; just let her go." I prayed to my heavenly Father, fervently asking him why and how this happened. I just could not comprehend how this could happen to such a smart, caring, and beautiful woman of God.

It appeared she was just abandoned, left with perfect strangers. I could tell she was not a threat to anyone. She was beautiful; she could play the piano. She just needed someone to believe in her and to take the time to help her. I watched her as we went to church together. There was a piano. I asked, "Mom, can you play this piano? She told me she used to but couldn't now. "Mom, sit down, open the hymnal, and play for Jesus." She sat down, back straight, shoulders back, and played like an angel.

The trouble was she felt abandoned. She had been separated from her one and only true love, my father. Even worse, she was separated from me, her only child. That's enough to throw anyone into deep depression. However at the time, my father made the decisions based on the guidance of doctors. In fact, my mother should have never been committed to such a facility. She could have been treated at home with love and proper Christian counseling. Today, doctors would never lock up someone like her in a mental institution. They would treat her with medication and counseling in the fleshly realm. However, according to God's work, she needed deliverance.

My mother came from a large house in Upstate New York, in a secure and stable environment. Then she married and moved to a small, remote rural location in West Virginia. So her entire world was completely changed. That would affect anyone. In addition to this, she just had a child and was dealing with all these challenges. She tried to go back to New York, where she last had complete peace. No one understood what she was experiencing. How deep is this, friend? Could you possibly be in this same situation yourself? Today she would probably be diagnosed with and treated for postpartum depression, not being crazy. Such a sad story. It hurts my heart so much to know this was her life.

My father loved her more than life itself. However, he was told by doctors that she was a hopeless cause. His heart was broken to the point he had a nervous breakdown. Because these doctors made bad decisions, three lives were destroyed, not just one. It has affected my life tremendously.

The moral of the story is go to God, not man. Man will let you down; God will not. The answer is not to hide the problem behind closed doors, run to a doctor to get medication, or run to alcohol or drugs to kill the pain. The internal pain must be dealt with up front through one's relationship with God. We must get to the root of the issue at hand and get rid of that toxicity so the poison can be erased from your soul. This results from fully surrendering yourself to your heavenly Father. Never bow to anyone except your heavenly Father. As you fully surrender to him and ask him for guidance and forgiveness of your sins, the door opens to the rest of your life. He then releases the keys to you, and you walk through the front door, not the back door because of shame. It is not God's desire for you to walk in shame or be forced into situations that make you feel less than. That comes from the enemy. Rebuke those thoughts and decisions. You truly have the right to live a good life. Not a mediocre life back in the corner, waiting for someone to approve your existence.

You see, friend, God made you and I for relationships. He made us to thrive through proper relationships. Can you imagine how my mother must have felt being jerked away from her husband she adored and her only child?

That's why I am writing this book, to reach out and help that one or the millions who never have the opportunities to know their worth.

As a little girl my heart was sick. The one thing I looked so forward to was my dad taking me to church and seeing him play and sing and laugh. He was the happiest when he played and sang. It was there in church, or anywhere he else played and sang, that he was truly at peace.

Life can be so unfair. But when we meet Jesus, everything changes. It's then you begin to uncover the gold inside you that you didn't know or even think existed. Life is not about what we get; it's truly about what we can give to others to help them become everything God created them to be.

Let's talk about what it means to have a personal relationship with our heavenly Father. Remember when you were a little child and couldn't wait to see your mommy and daddy first thing in the morning, after you awakened from a night of blissful dreams? Well let me share with you what the Holy Bible says. It tells us that all who call in the name of the Lord and believe with all their hearts that Jesus is Lord of their lives shall be saved. It's the same with your heavenly Father. He longs to see your face; he longs to hear your voice. He longs to fellowship with you every second of every day. It's there that you find supernatural peace and understanding. It's there you are truly embraced by the pure love of our risen Savior, Jesus!

Let us embrace that even more throughout this book. Let us open our spiritual eyes and invite the beautiful Holy Ghost in to take the rights of our lives in every area. The Holy Ghost led me as I wrote this book. Let this be your book for your precious children, to bring them closer to you.

Let's all agree from this moment forward as we read this book, we will focus on you, Lord. We will journal our thoughts. We will pray for each other daily so that we will all benefit from this journey.

So dear friends, get your notepads, your pens, and your glass of water, and let's go. We have a trail to blaze for Jesus.

Heavenly Father, we thank you for downloading from heaven right now your exact blueprint for our lives. We thank you for strategically linking us with the right mates, the right pastors, and the right friends and mentors to take us higher unto you.

Heavenly Father, we adore you. There is none like you—none before you and none after you. We come together in one accord completely surrendered unto you for your glory.

Our lives are not our own; to you we belong. We give ourselves to you. Use us, mold us, and transform us. Let us truly be your image so that we may take your good news out to a lost and dying world.

When looking in the mirror, what do you see? Do you see the beautiful person you truly are? Or do you see someone struggling from within? Are you happy with what you see? Would you like to be more vibrant, more radiant? Pour into the person you see in that mirror so that you can truly overflow and pour into others.

There is gold inside you. At times I'm sure you don't see it. That's the enemy trying to tell you that you're not good enough. Jesus says you are more than good enough. Jesus qualifies you, friend.

Not a man, not a woman, not your pastor, no one qualifies or loves you like Jesus. Nobody loves you like Jesus. Grasp that in your beautiful mind. When the world falls apart, you have Jesus. Run to him, not man. When you wake up, run or walk with Jesus. I find it so invigorating to start my day off walking and running with Jesus. He is my best friend, lover of my soul. There is so much purity in that. It's a pure, sound invigorating love. That embraces me every morning as I wake, as I open my eyes and do my little stretch. I begin my day by thanking my heavenly Father for waking me up. He so deserves the first part of our day. The first part of everything. Let the river of God's love in and through you. Be an unending conduit of his pure agape love to everyone you meet. As you do, walls will fall, hearts will open, and deep inner healing will happen.

Lay it all down with him. It is my desire for each of you to be totally free and to feel the warmth of his embrace. He is all I want. He is all I've ever needed. Lord, help us know you are real and near. Draw each person reading this close to you, Lord.

Friend, nothing in this life is more important than your one-on-one relationship with your heavenly Father. As you build that relationship and truly abide in him, you will then be able to love your God-given mate with the true real love that never ends.

As you read this, I want you to decide inside yourself that you are going to make today and every day the greatest events of your lifetime. Do not be passive today. You are alive! Act like it! Celebrate yourself! Stop and smell the roses today! Dance that dance today! Run that marathon! Dare to love and dance again! Go forward with joy and great boldness.

I dedicate this book to my Lord and Savior, heavenly Father, Jesus Christ. Lover of my soul, my best friend, encourager. To my loving children—Hunter, Hayden, and Landen—thank you for never giving up on me and always encouraging me to be me. Although I have suffered from many tragedies, you have always been faithful, always. I marvel in your goodness and mercy. I long to forever be in your presence. I would like to thank as well my dad, who taught me how truly to worship and show kindness like Jesus.

1

Your Troubles

Prayer

Jump in for a word of encouragement and prayer. Let us unite in prayer and supplication across this great nation. What a lovely day it is out there when we give God total control of our lives. No matter what is going on right now in your life, I want you to know that God is right there in the middle of your situation. He is right there waiting for you to surrender unto him. He is your Papa God, the One who loves you unconditionally.

Let us come together in worship and praise and lift holy hands to heaven. Papa, we have come to honor you; we have come to give you the respect and the glory that you so deserve. We thank you for opening the floodgates of heaven and releasing a fresh outpouring of your Holy Spirit presence to each one reading this book. You're not reading this by mistake but by divine appointment. I pray that after reading this book you will be transformed by the renewing of your mind. I believe that God is doing a new thing in you right now, as it states in Isaiah 43:18–21:

> Remember ye not the former things, neither consider
> the things of old.

Behold, I will do a new thing; now it shall spring forth; shall ye not know it? I will even make a way in the wilderness, and rivers in the desert.

The beast of the field shall honor me, the dragons and the owls: because I give waters in the wilderness, and rivers in the desert, to give drink to my people, my chosen.

This people have I formed for myself; they shall shew forth my praise.

If you feel somewhat disgusted and overwhelmed by an aspect of your life, you're in the best place for change. Frustration is a sign of vision. Being overwhelmed can lead to a major life change. Although we don't normally equate the word "disgust" with positive action, being sick and tired of your current circumstances is a clear sign that it's time for a positive change! This book is about taking 100 percent responsibility for where you are and where you're headed from this point forward. As you read along you will develop the essential skill needed to achieve life's success—self-discipline. Self-discipline is the key to self-fulfillment. You, too, can be an overachiever if you implement self-discipline on a daily basis. I encourage you to ask the Lord to release unto you the right accountability partner to help you achieve your daily goals.

Thank you for taking this time with me and your Papa God, your precious friend. The main key I release unto you now is to take control of your daily habits. God works in seasons, patterns, and cycles. Realizing his timing is key to activating his greatest blessings in your life. Your life will change with obedience to God! No more missed moments in your life, precious friend.

Message

As we go through life, we go through storms. The Lord expects you to be patient. I listen to phone calls from people reaching out to me about how to deal with this, how to deal with that, what to do with this, and what to do with that. I asked the Lord how to answer all your questions, and he told me that no matter what, he expects us to reach out to him and to do the right thing. First, grab your Bible and then sit down and read it. Look up the scriptures pertaining to your situation, and go to him. You know, we all go through many kinds of scenarios, and we have free will. It is ours to make the right choice because the lives you and I choose to live may be the only Bible some people may ever read. This so important.

I stopped and prayed. I asked the Lord how to handle situations because we all face them. We all go through troubles. There are times we just simply don't know what to do.

Since I have been dealing with teenagers, I understand everyone is real. I understand that, but you have to get back to what is right; you have to get back to what the Bible says about that. You must teach your children exactly what is said in the Bible about how important it is to maintain your holiness, and how important it is that they realize they are also special to the Lord and should follow what he says. Let's understand. We all go through it, but we have to do what is right. And we must answer to the Lord for ourselves.

"Here, so we are going to talk about how to watch for God to appear to you on the troubled waters of struggling. Be not afraid (Matthew 14:27). The first step in getting through the struggles of your life is to practice doing what you can do first. It is grounded in your thinking that God expects you to do what you can. He is always going forward. So God expects you and I to do what we can do.

The next step is to be aware when things start getting out of control. Watch for danger signals and red flags. You are at a point of need, and it is at this point of need when God will appear to you without failure. He will appear to do what only he can do. He will show up just when you least expect it. That means a miracle is about to appear before you. When you do everything you can and you release it unto the Lord, your miracle will come to you.

Do you believe this? Do you really believe that God answers your prayers? Do you believe what his Word says? You need to ask yourself, "Is there anything in me that is not right?"

It is time to search yourself and say, "Dear heavenly Father, if there is anything in me or I have made any mistakes or I handled anything wrong, forgive me. I ask that you would wash me, cleanse me, and fill me afresh and anew with your beautiful Holy Spirit."

Will you try to practice believing it? This is a practice I have engaged in for many years. I continually remind myself that God always appears to me at the point of my need. And he appears to other people at their points of need over and over. He wants you to expect him to answer your prayers. So God expects you to expect him to appear to you at the point of your need. But your point of need is not the only time God may appear in some form of help to you. He is a sovereign God, and he can and does appear as he wills.

From the moment you were conceived in your mother's womb, you have been very precious to the heavenly Father. You are all diamonds to him. He longs for you to have the best life that you possibly can have because he is a God of love, and he does not want anybody left behind. He brought me here at this particular moment because I care about your spirituality. And he wants you to know that whatever situation you are in, if you surrender unto him, if you get down on your knees wherever you are and surrender unto him, asking for forgiveness for your sins and your wrongdoings, he will turn your mess into a miracle. He really will. But you must surrender everything unto him. You have got to stay with your heavenly Father, and anytime you are out of alignment, ask him to bring you back into order.

So let us say the beginning of the Lord's Prayer together: "Our Father, who art in heaven, Hallowed be thy Name. Thy kingdom come. Thy will be done on Earth, as it is in heaven."

What we see is the Lord's desire for us to be free from torment, free from disease, free from sickness, free from pain, free from worry, and free from anxiety. So if you have been worrying about yourself, rebuke that which is not of the Lord.

God is love, and he longs for you to surrender everything and ask him to come into your heart to wash you, to cleanse you, and to fill you. God wants me to expect him to appear at the point of my need. So God wants you to believe 100 percent that when you pray, he is going to answer your prayer. God is right here with me amid any storm to give me my miracles. You have got to believe that no matter what, he is right there to release you into your *miracle*. He loves you so much that he sent his only Son, Jesus, to the cross for you so that you could be free of all that debris, free from all that sorrow, free from all that pain, free from the relationship issues, and free from disease.

He adores you because you are so beautiful to him. You are all diamonds, and there is gold in all of you. He just simply wants you to search yourself. Ask yourself, "Is there anything in me that is not of the Lord? Is there anything in me that I need to repent of? Is there anything that I need to ask forgiveness for?" If there is, now is the time to surrender to your heavenly Father. Ask him to come into your heart and wash you or cleanse you. I promise he will make you feel that you have a fresh look.

Do not wallow in self-pity; do not wallow on the past. You are more than that. Jesus was not a baby; Jesus was not a complainer. Jesus was a man of great wisdom, of boldness, humility. And most of all, of unconditional love.

He expects us to be the best models we can possibly be. And friend, he gave you and I his best, so shouldn't you and I give him our best?

Hallelujah.

You can talk to Jesus right in the middle of anything. He longs to be your best friend, and he longs to hear all of your cares. Whatever it is that is on your mind, that is boggling you down today, Jesus wants you to tell him. Go for a little walk with him. Go to your special room in your home, wherever your altar is, and surrender unto him. Tell him what is going on because Jesus loves to hear everything, and he wants to help you. You just have to talk to him.

You have not because you ask not, seek and you shall find, knock and the door shall open. You can talk to Jesus amid anything, and he will come into your situations. Didn't Jesus and Peter speak to each other? It was a relatively short conversation. Have you ever noticed that there is not always time for a lot of words in a storm, and that you do not need a lot of words? Sometimes when you talk too much, you and others might get overwhelmed. So you simply need to be brief.

Tell him you need a miracle, and say it with all boldness. You need to be able to walk on top of the storm right into the safe arms of Jesus Christ. Jesus is extending his arms to you, friend. Whatever situation you are going through, just go into his arms, and let Jesus hold you, let Jesus take care of all these issues. You were not made to carry worry, you were not made to carry pain, and you were not made to carry anxiety. The Lord wants to set you free from that. Receive that tonight in the name of Jesus. Everything that is not of God must bow to the name above all names, the name of Jesus Christ. Hallelujah.

You need to look at things in the spiritual realm. You are looking at things in the natural, and you see nothing that makes you cheerful. But the Lord brought me here, friend, to tell you that he is there with you. He is extending his hand to you right now. He will come walking to you on waters of your troubles and speak words of cheer to you. His words are usually simple. All his sentences are short, but his words are spirit, and they are life. He is the very nail of your life to start giving you the miracle you need.

God brings people into your life for divine reasons. So when God brings you special people, honor them. And honor those relationships. Being special is God's best quality. He wants all his children to feel special because you *are* very special. He delights in being special to you and in making you special too.

He is happy when you are happy. He is happy when you are smiling. He is happy when you are dancing, and he is happy when you are sharing your testimony of how far he has brought you.

There are moments when you must choose to expect God to do what he can do. You truly have to expect it. You have to believe it 100 percent that he is going to do what you are asking him to do. Don't be afraid to pray. I promise when you do what you can do, you can then expect God to do what he can do. You will form a new partnership between yourself and your heavenly Father, a miracle partnership.

Get on top of this problem instead of having it stay on top of you and destroy you. Walk on it, and it will be a miracle. This miracle will happen to you, and you will make it. There is nothing that God won't do to help his children only if they surrender unto Him.

The thrill of making it through will make you a new person. One who has faced the worst and is successfully going through it looks back on it with a powerful new partnership with God. That is what God wants. God wants a partnership, a relationship with all of you. So search yourself right now, friend. If there is anything in you that is not of God, if you made some wrong decisions, simply surrender, ask for forgiveness, and let us all strive to be better people, to be the best we can be because of what Jesus has done for you. He paid the ultimate price.

Father could have said, "They are not worth it." Instead, he turned his back and let his only precious Son go to that cross for you. Shouldn't you and I really give him our best in everything that we do? Shouldn't we? Shouldn't we truly give our heavenly Father our best because that was his only son?

Can you imagine giving up your only son and watching your only son stretch his arms out and take that much pain? Can you imagine your only son having thorns in his head, being spat upon, and being blasphemed?

So it is time that you and I step up. It is time that you and I examine ourselves. Is there anything in us that we need to get rid of? Is there any darkness in us? Is there anything that you and I are doing wrong? God take us deeper unto you and surround us with your Holy angels.

Father God, we thank you for opening divine doors. Father, we thank you for divine and accountable partners. Father, we thank you for divine relationships. Father, we thank you for Holy Ghost–filled pastors, mentors, coaches, and friends. Lord, we bless your name.

I want you to ask yourself a nice question: What can I do when things start getting out of control? Tell God your need, and he will always come to you at the point of your need. He will come if you just surrender unto him.

I want to hear your testimonies. The elderly matter the same as you, and they have so much wisdom to share. Friend, I want you to make a pact with me that within the next seven days, you are going to make an oath to grab your Bible and maybe some kind of little gift, whatever gift you find, find an elderly person, go read the Bible to them, and pray with them. And you will make sure that they are safe because the elderly are so precious. God is really laying the elderly on my heart. You know you are not old till you are ninety-seven; that's what I say. I want you to reach out to the older people; give them the respect and honor they deserve. Honor your mother and father. Even if you don't fully agree with your parents, take the time to check on them. Take the time to make sure they are okay. Take the time to say, "Hey, Mom and Dad, I love you. You are in my thoughts, and I am praying for you. Is there anything I can pray for you about?" When you honor your mother and father, God respects that. Honor your pastors, honor the people who take the time to pray for you, and honor the people who take the time to love you.

Heavenly Father, we humbly come before the throne of grace to give you the honor, the praise, and the respect that you so deserve because you love us so much. Heavenly Father, we adore you. We thank you for life. I thank you, Lord, that you are opening the floodgates of heaven and releasing a special encounter to each and every person reading this. I thank you, Lord, that you're opening their spiritual eyes to receive your love, to receive your peace, and to receive your healing in the name of Jesus. I decree and declare you are going from victory to victory, strength to strength, glory to glory, and you will be the lender and not the borrower. Don't get in over your head. Remember to tithe; remember to give first fruits to your heavenly Father.

And if you are blessed by this ministry and would like to partner with this ministry, you may do so by going to joytodayministries.com and clicking donate at any time. When you sow your seed, miracles will continue to flow your way in the name of Jesus. So at this time I give you time to hop on there and donate. Become a partner with us; help

2

The Power of Forgiveness

Prayer

I am DeSerio with Joy Today Ministries coming on for a word of encouragement and prayer for you.

> Dear Lord, we have come to honor you. We come to give you the respect and the glory that you so deserve. You are the most kind and gracious God. We thank you for opening the floodgates of heaven and releasing a fresh outpouring of your Holy Spirit. I thank you that you are releasing a heavenly atmosphere to everyone reading. Father, I thank you. We thank you, Lord. I thank you, Lord, for releasing your words from heaven and being there for your beautiful family. Amen.

Message

I want to talk to you about something important. The Lord laid it on my heart to reiterate about the power of forgiveness. You know, when we go through difficult situations, there can be unforgiveness, bitterness, and wrong words said. The Lord laid it to me to let everyone who needs to hear that today you are set free from words of unforgiveness, hurtful words, and for being in religion instead of in relationship with your heavenly Father.

The redemptive power of God is released when people forgive each other. Individuals, families, churches, and even the atmosphere of a city can change when pardon is released. When such a display of grace is poured out, principalities and powers are neutralized, often without so much as speaking a word against the other. So whoever it is that has wronged you, the Lord wants you to forgive completely. Forgiveness is at the core and is the essence of a relationship with the Father.

The Bible itself says that whenever pardon is given, there is a definite and occasional dramatic release of life against the power of death. Heavenly places observed the release of life when Jesus on the cross prayed, "Father forgive them for they know not what they do." The Lord wants you to do the same thing; truly forgive anybody in your life you feel has been against you. The Lord brought me here to tell you it's not worth it.

Sometimes we get caught up in emotions. The Lord wants to set you free. Remember when Jesus was on the cross, He canceled our certificates of debt through his act of forgiveness. He simultaneously disarmed the rulers and authorities according to Colossians 2:14:15. Likewise, when we forgive, there's a canceling of debts. He wants to disarm the enemy and give you life. How does he do that? He does that when you surrender, forgive, and let it all go unto him. And once you ask for forgiveness and simply let it go, it is gone. The Lord wants to do a new thing in your life. Jeremiah 29:11 tells us that he has a plan for us.

It is likely that such words as "wonderful" and "glorious" were used to describe the baptism of the love that was released. Perhaps that person didn't even understand what you were trying to say or didn't understand your text message or email. And you have harbored hard feelings against this person. The Lord wants you to cast that unforgiveness upon him. Can we see that forgiveness is the very heart of Jesus Christ?

We need to remember that no matter what you are going through, the proper procedure is to forgive because God wants our pure hearts. He wants you to cast that unforgiveness and bitterness to him, and simply say, "Father, forgive me for mistaking somebody. Forgiveness for misunderstanding that person, Father. I don't even really understand what happened, but today I wish to be set free. Today I cast all that over to you. Heavenly Father, I thank you for releasing healing, releasing love, that pure agape love from heaven, And I thank you, Lord God, for releasing supernatural healing to me."

The power is in forgiveness. It is when you forgive that person and set free that the Lord will set you free. Hallelujah.

The Lord brought me here to let you know that hell is real and that he loves you very much. He wants you to understand that today is your day to be totally set free from anxiety and tormenting spirits. He died on that cross so you could be free from everything, so receive the freedom right now, friend, in the mighty name of Jesus Christ.

It is time that we bow before the throne of grace and lift our holy hands to heaven as we give our precious heavenly Father the honor, the praise, and the glory he so deserves. We are to model and be the image of Jesus Christ. In order to do that, we have to stop the stinking thinking and we be single-minded. You see, we are to be the images of Christ. And remember, Jesus was a man of compassion and love. He was a man of boldness. He was a doer, and he always went forward. So friend, I am here to tell you that the Lord has heard your complaints, your heart cries, and all your prayers. This is your chance. If you've never accepted Jesus Christ into your heart, now is the time to simply say it:

> Dear heavenly Father, I repent of my sins, and I acknowledge that you sent your only Son, Jesus, to the cross. I thank you, Lord, for turning my heart into a heart full of love, peace, and joy. Fill me with the precious Holy Spirit, and create in me boldness to read my Bible, to pray, and to go forward in my life.

If you said that prayer, welcome to the family of God. That is the greatest decision you could ever make, to ask Jesus into your heart, to ask the Holy Spirit to wash you, to cleanse you and fill you afresh. Grab a Bible and start reading it every day. Read that Bible, worship, pray, and thank God for his goodness. Hallelujah.

Thank you, friend, for reading and spending a little bit of your time with me. Visit Joy Today Ministries today. God bless you, bless your family, bless your ministry, and bless your business.

The scripture the Lord laid on my heart is Matthew 9:12, 13. On hearing this, Jesus said, "It is not the healthy who need a doctor but the sick. Go and learn what this means: 'I desire mercy not sacrifice for I have not come to call the righteous but sinners.'"

Jesus came for you, for that one person who doesn't know him. Jesus came to set everybody free so that everyone would have the opportunity to repent, be set free, and go to heaven. Jesus was a man of so much compassion and love. Receive that love today. Receive that healing and compassion, and ask Jesus to come into your heart and renew your relationship with your heavenly Father.

Your relationship with your heavenly Father is the most important relationship that you could ever have, and it begins by surrendering and committing to him 100 percent. He knows what is best for you and longs to hear your voice. He wants to see you happy, and he longs to bless you.

You see, from birth to death we go through a test, and I want you and I to make the right decisions. That begins by opening the Bible and reading it on a day-to-day basis. Read it aloud to your spouse, to your children, and to the elderly. May God richly bless you. Remember that your heavenly Father totally adores you, and he is in love with you.

If you feel led to partner with this ministry, please do so by going to joytodayministries.com and clicking donate.

God richly bless you, bless your family, and bless your ministry. Remember that there is no need to fear any sickness because everything must bow to the name of Jesus Christ. Cancer must bow to the name of Jesus, heart disease must bow to the name of Jesus, liver disease must bow to the name of Jesus, and addiction to porn must bow to the name of Jesus. It is not worth losing your soul. God wants to bless you, friend, but you have to start being holy. You have to be careful what you allow in your mind, in your eyes, and inside your body. Your body is the temple of the Most High God, and you must honor your heavenly Father with your body by taking care of yourself. Choose your friends and relationships wisely.

The Lord will honor you; he will bless you. He will bless your union. He will bless your marriage and your relationships. And he will bless your life.

He is taking you to higher places and to a new level tonight. Keep your feet on the solid foundation of the gospel of Jesus Christ. Hallelujah.

3

Your Emotions

Prayer

Let us join together in prayer and supplication.

Dear most kind and gracious heavenly Father, we come before the throne of grace, lifting our holy hands to heaven, thanking you, Lord, for the privilege and the opportunity to be able to pray. We thank you, Lord, that you love us enough that we can unite, and we can pray and read your Word. Glory to your name.

Message

We're going to talk about emotions today. A lot of people contacted me the past few days about their emotions. You see, those who lack control over their emotions are in danger of sabotaging the fulfillment of their destinies. Friend, the Lord brought me here to pray with you and to help you learn how to take control of your emotions. Your thoughts, your visions, and your perceptions produce feelings or emotions that are also part of your soul. For example, if you were to think about a fun memory from your past, it might produce a light and happy feeling. If you were to imagine getting a raise at work, you might feel excited. On the other hand, if you were to think about a thief breaking into your home, you can experience feelings of fear, anxiety, or terror. That is because your thoughts produce feelings. If you have feelings, there are thoughts behind them, whether you are aware of them or not.

Feelings or emotions are part of your soul's functions, so you need to get your emotions intact. How you feel about things produces a manifestation of what those feelings represent. Remember what it says in Job 3:25: what I fear comes upon me. It is not enough to simply have mental agreement with a promising God's Word. For example, I might agree in mind that God can cause a person to come out of their wheelchair and walk, but when I look at the person in the chair, my mind is challenged by what I see, and it produces feelings that are full of doubt. I am more likely to believe my feelings at that moment because my mind became doubtful and anxious, and my emotions reinforced that belief. What you feel is a powerful influence on what you believe.

I know many people generally say that God is good, yet they do not see God's goodness manifest in their lives. As a result they tell me things like, "I don't feel good," "I don't feel the love," "I don't see the goodness," "I don't see the joy." They doubt that God is near to them. They doubt that he loves them and desires to show them his goodness. Somewhere behind that feeling is a thought, and the Lord brought me here to tell you that he loves you. If you are in this situation, we are going to pray over you and tell your emotions to bow to the name of Jesus coming to full alignment.

The person who agrees with the Bible and believes that God is good, that God is a rewarder to those who diligently seek him, may also hold a belief to the contrary, that "Maybe he doesn't want to show me goodness because I'm not worthy." If that is you, and you think you are not worthy, remember that is a lie straight from the enemy, the one who generates negative feelings. The one that tampers with your good feelings will reveal and reinforce your predominant thoughts and beliefs.

Our senses are important because they are rightly aligned with God's truth. They will produce prosperity in your soul, which will attract to you what you are feeling. Many scriptures speak about the heart, but in the Bible, "heart" is often another word used for your soul. The heart, your emotions, feelings, thoughts, imagination, and will need to be cared for and nurtured so that you can live a life of prosperity and good health. "Watch over your heart with all diligence; For from it flow the Springs of Life" (Proverbs 4:23).

Your first response to something can set a lasting tone. When you're extremely tired, it's sometimes best not to talk to someone about things that are really bothering you. Your words might come across harsh and not as intended. So it's wise to pray before you speak and choose your words wisely.

Business leaders are aware that first impressions are extremely important. They know it is important to have a good initial feeling in order for their products or businesses to be accepted. For example, you might go to a restaurant that makes the best chicken dinner in town, but if you are not treated well at the door, you don't care how the food tastes because you were disrespected. Even if the food was good, you will likely not remember how great that chicken tasted because we all want to be respected. We all want to have good customer service. Whenever someone mentions the name of the restaurant, you will recall that bad feeling, that bad service, and word of mouth can make or destroy a person's business or character. I remember once ordering breakfast at a restaurant. When I ate the first bite of the egg, it tasted fishy, it turned my mouth, and I spat out the egg on the plate. My entire body felt distressed and repulsed. I never again went to that restaurant.

Every time I see one of those chain restaurants, my memory of that experience kicks in, and I drive right by it. So it's very important that we take the time to pray. And then we need to take the time to give our best, to do our best in our ministries or businesses whenever we are serving the Lord's people, whether it is at a conference, in a church service, on television program, or evangelizing. I encourage our team on the street to create a favorable first experience for the people. The feeling they initially have will attract more of the same throughout the events or the encounter.

That's what the Lord brought me here to tell you; first impressions really matter. But even if you goof up, are a knucklehead, and say some things you shouldn't say, if you pray and ask the heavenly Father to help you get your emotions in line, he will. It is important that you, "watch over your heart with all diligence for from it flows the Springs of Life" (Proverbs 4:23).

It is important to watch your word every day. It is important that you work out daily. It is important that you pray every day. I just heard the Lord say that you should release everything to him. As you go about your day, release all your cares, all your worries, all your anxieties to your heavenly Father.

Do not be passive about every day of your life. You are alive, friend. Act like it, talk like it, celebrate yourself, celebrate life, speak a little louder, speak a little faster, smile bigger, laugh louder, tell that someone who means so much to you how much he or she means to you. Honor the people God places in your life to help you. And make sure that you use wisdom when you need wisdom. Ask the Lord for wisdom.

"This is the day which the Lord hath made, we will rejoice and be glad in it" (Psalm 118:24).

Keep walking. Walk through whatever it is you're going through in life. Picture yourself driving in a heavy hailstorm. You don't stop. You keep driving knowing you will move out of the storm's range.

Remember Joseph? Remember David? Every day of adversity was simply a stepping-stone toward the throne. Keep walking, friend. No matter what you are going through, keep going forward. Remember seasons change, people change, attacks don't last forever, weather changes, circumstances change, so don't be discouraged about something. Maybe you goofed up today. Maybe you said something or did something you shouldn't have. Simply repent. Ask the Lord for forgiveness, shake it off, and move forward. Expect the supernatural power of God every day.

Jesus invested his first thirty years in preparation for his ministry. So we must prepare for life. If we fail to prepare, we set ourselves up for failure. Moses spent eighty years becoming a great leader. Time is your friend, so don't hurry. Slow down, enjoy the journey. Remember, patience is the weapon that forces deception to reveal itself. "Weeping may endure for a night, but joy cometh in the morning" (Psalm 30:5).

> I will be with thee saith the Lord, through the rivers, they shall not overflow thee.
>
> When you walk through the fire thou shall not be burned. Neither shall they flame candle under thee, for I am the Lord thy God. (Isaiah 43:2, 3)

Whatever the situation is, ask the Lord to pull out its root, cut it off with an axe, burn it up with the Holy Spirit, and release love and healing inside you. By the stripes of Jesus you are saved. There is no problem too big that your heavenly Father cannot help you figure it out. It is a matter of believing. Hallelujah.

You need to know that you are important to the Lord. All of you are very important. Your worth and significance are determined by the kinds of problems you're solving for someone. If you want to earn a hundred dollars an hour, you must find a hundred-dollars-an-hour-problem to solve. You aren't like others. We all have special callings. Find what makes you different, and solve a problem with it. Prosperity is inevitable. One of the master keys to personal miracles is to get involved with the needs of others, to get your thoughts off yourself, and find someone to blast. Somebody out there needs what you have; somebody out there is praying for you in their life.

Joseph used his gift of interpreting dreams to help the tormented pharaoh. He was promoted from the prison to the palace. Joseph prayed for his friends during the worst crisis of his life.

God bless each and every one of you. Remember the Lord loves you, and before you speak, stop and pray and ask yourself, "What would Jesus do?" "How would Jesus handle the situation?"

Friend, we just don't understand what another person is going through. Instead of overthinking and being double-minded, intercede in prayer for that person, pray for their peace, happiness, prosperity and pray for their divine relationships. The greatest thing that you can do for people is to pray for them.

Tell someone what Jesus has done for you. The first two letters of the word "gospel" spell "go." Christianity is a network of activity, so promote Jesus today. When you promote Jesus, you can never go wrong because when you stand tall for Jesus, he will stand tall for you. You are the creation. He is your Creator. You cannot out-think the One who made you. He was delighted in performing the impossible when he created you.

He is the master of the turnaround. Jesus has made the difference in your life. Tell someone about it today. Tell somebody what Jesus has done for you.

> Go ye into all the world and preach the gospel to every creature and these signs shall follow them that believe in my name. They shall speak with new tongues. They shall take up serpents, and if they drink any deadly thing it shall not hurt them. They shall lay hands on the sick and they shall recover. (Mark 16:15–18)

Start pursuing the wisdom of God. Get into the Word of God. Give him ten to twenty more minutes of your time, and watch what he will do for you. Wisdom opens doors, and wisdom opens prosperity. When you don't know what to do, you can pray for wisdom, and you'll get it.

Jesus had made unto us the wisdom of God. Whatever you face, just do what you know Jesus would do. Jesus said you have received two gifts from God: your mouth and wisdom. Unexpected things may happen; it is called life. Don't worry or fret. Don't second-guess yourself. Don't spend your whole life saying, "I'm sorry." Remember, Jesus was no wimp. He didn't go around saying he was sorry. Jesus was humble, but he was bold and a man of few words. Someone greater than you is within you. Depend on him.

Get wisdom and understanding. Let it not depart from the words of my mouth (Proverbs 4:5). The length of days is in her right hand, and in her left hand, riches and honor (Proverbs 3:16). And like I said, face any problem that you may have honestly.

Go to the throne of grace. Kneel and pray. If you are confused, if you don't understand something, get on your knees and pray. Ask the Lord to help, so you'll understand what's going on. Release it to God. We weren't made to carry worry, anxiety, and torment. The Lord doesn't want that for you. So tonight, surrender it all into your heavenly Father's hands. It is Jesus. I hand you all my baggage. I choose to be happy. I choose to be at peace. I choose to be joyous and thankful because he stretched out his arms and died on the cross so that you and I could be free from all sin, free from confusion, free from anger, free from murmuring. All of us are going through different things in our lives, and sometimes we don't understand. That is why the best thing you can do when you don't understand something is simply to pray for others. Like I said, pray for their peace, pray for their happiness, pray for their family, pray for their prosperity. And watch what God would do for you because when you put others first and pray for them, you change the situation.

I have an important question to ask you. If you were to die this very second, do you know without a shadow of a doubt that you would go to heaven? If you can say yes to that question, that's totally awesome. But if you are not so sure, or maybe you have made some mistakes, or maybe you know you have backslidden, now is the time because he is real. The Lord cared enough about you to let you know that you have a Savior, and his name is Jesus. What you need to do is surrender. Wherever you are, say,

Dear heavenly Father, I made some mistakes in my life, and I ask for forgiveness. I acknowledge that you sent Jesus Christ, your only Son, to the cross. I ask that you forgive me, wash me, and fill me afresh with your Holy Spirit.

If you said that, friend, welcome to the family of God. The next step for you is to get a Bible and start reading it daily. Pray and get into a good church—a Holy Ghost–filled church, with a good pastor.

I want you to remember we are to first seek the kingdom of God and his righteousness. Then all these things will be added unto you (Matthew 6:33). When you don't know what to do, don't settle for second-best. Pray, fast, ask the Lord, and get in your prayer closet. If you are in a situation where you don't know what to do, get in their prayer closet fast, and pray for three days. Write down what you are praying for and go over that prayer every day. Decree and declare; speak it into existence. If you're praying for a promotion, if you're praying for a business, if you're praying to start a ministry, if you're praying to find your lifelong mates, write down what you want, and pray over it. And when God brings it to you, don't run away from it. Accept it and thank the Lord for it. Don't walk in fear. If you prayed for something and when God brings it, you get scared because you prayed and it happened. Don't run. Just thank him.

This job or ministry, whatever it is that you have not, you need to ask. Don't be afraid to talk to your heavenly Father. God richly blesses each and every one of us. God bless you; rest in the presence of the Lord. I bless you. I bless your family. I bless your ministry. I thank you, Lord, for releasing a heaven-like atmosphere to every home out there. I thank you for releasing ministering angels to every home. I thank you, Lord, that you are covering them. You are their shield; you are their protector. No harm shall come near their dwellings. You are blessed, friend. You are highly favored and walking in the supernatural power of God. Rest in the presence of the Lord tonight.

When you wake up in the morning, be refreshed with joy. Praise the Lord, and decree and declare that your day is going to be victorious, the best day yet. God, richly bless each and every one of you.

If you feel led to sow into this ministry, you may do so by going to joytodayministries.com and click donate. God bless you all.

4

Winning Every Battle

Prayer

Let's join together in prayer and supplication:

Kind and gracious Father, we have come to worship you. We have come to give you honor. We have come to give you praise. We have come to break down the dividing walls. Thank you, Father, for the honor to be able to pray and the honor to be able to worship.

Come let us give the heavenly Father the honor, the praise, the worship, and the respect he deserves for he is good, so gracious, and so awesome. Second Chronicles 16:9 tells us, "For the eyes of the Lord move to and fro throughout the Earth that He may strongly support those whose heart is completely His." Amen.

Message

So in case someone has never told you, you have a heavenly Father who totally adores you, and he is bringing me here to encourage you, to say

God bless you, and let you know that you're very important. You're a very important part of the body of Christ, and we have come to let you know that the Lord has a plan for your life. I don't know if anyone has ever told you that Jesus has a great plan for your life, but he brought me here this morning to tell you that all of you are very precious in the sight of the Lord. He has a plan and a purpose for everyone, and we have to put on the full armor of God.

A prepared soldier never goes into battle without the appropriate armor and weapons. The potential for victory of spiritual battle hinges on having suitable armor and weapon for deliverance. A spiritual warfare is described in Ephesians 6. So grab your Bible, your pad, and pen. Let's thank him for his goodness. Let us unite in one accord across this great globe for his glory. Let us give him the praise, the honor, and the glory that he deserves. He woke you and me up. He deserves our praise.

First of all, it tells us in full detail in Ephesians 6 that we must put on the full armor of God. You should fill your mind with the Word of God. Fill your mind with the Word of God. Reading and meditating on the Bible protects you in the Christian walk. That's why he says we need to renew our minds daily with the washing of his Word. That's why he wants you and I to give him our whole hearts, which are protected by the breastplate, so that we can have that intimate relationship with him.

How important is the Word of God? Do you know how important the Word of God is, friend? It is very important, isn't it? If we didn't have the Word of God, we wouldn't have the sword to protect ourselves with. In order to know who we are in Christ, speaking the Word aloud is vital in preparation of the gospel of peace. The Word of God must affect your walk on your life.

This happens as the Bible fills your mind, and your mouth touches your heart and manifests or is seen in your daily routine. Your daily routine influences your heart with truth and the shield of faith to stay armed with the Word of God.

Read the Word of God aloud with boldness, and then put on the helmet of salvation. In the natural, the helmet protects the head from injury, while the helmet of salvation deals with your nature, your character, and your doctrine. Knowing God's Word makes you ballast, stable, and prepared. That's why we need to start off the day and praising and worshipping Him.

Washing our minds with the Word of God is vital. As your life becomes strong and established, the sword of the Spirit becomes an offensive weapon—not a defensive weapon—against the enemy. The enemy feels the power of the Most High. You're able to stand victoriously against the evil one and his army. Hallelujah. Open your heart today, and let Jesus in your heart 100 percent. All you have to do is surrender unto your heavenly Father and say, "Dear heavenly Father, I need you. I need you in my heart. Turn my stony heart into a flesh heart full of your pure agape love. Wash me and cleanse me. Fill me afresh and anew with your precious, beautiful Holy Spirit." If you said that prayer from your heart, welcome to the family of God. That is the greatest decision that you could ever make. That's the cry of my heart today, friend, for me to know without a shadow of a doubt that you love the Lord and that you can do this. You can open doors by your prayer and your supplication. You're studying, and that's important.

I came to let you know that you matter, and even though you're taking the smallest step of faith, God will still intercede. He'll take your hand and walk you through it. I want to let you know that you matter; everyone matters. If you just take a small step of faith and ask for forgiveness for your sins or anything that you've done wrong, and if you renew your covenant with Him, the Lord will honor that because he rewards those who diligently seek him. He's looking for a pure heart full of love from heaven, and that's what he wants to do for you. Today he wants to wash you, he wants to cleanse you, he wants to feel you afresh and anew with his beautiful Holy Spirit. It's because he loves you so much that he sent his only Son, Jesus, to the cross to die for you. That's why we must put on the full armor of God not once a week or a month but daily. We must always pray with all power and supplication in the Spirit.

Do you want to make the divine connection with God today?

Then you simply just need to ask him to come into your heart and ask Jesus to come into your heart to wash you, cleanse you, and fill you afresh and anew with the beautiful Holy Spirit.

Don't pray to escape your trouble. Don't pray to be comfortable in your emotions. Pray to do the will of God in every situation. We need to pray for the Father's will to be done and ask the beautiful Holy Spirit to lead and guide every thought, everything that we do in our lives. My prayer for you, friend, is that you simply surrender 100 percent to your heavenly Father and say, "Father, I made a mess of things. But I know that you sent Jesus Christ, your only Son, to the cross. Come into my heart. Forgive me of my sins. Wash me and cleanse me; fill me afresh and anew with your beautiful Holy Spirit." And once again, if you said that prayer, welcome to the family of God. That is the greatest decision that you could ever make. Hallelujah. We must come before God with thanksgiving.

All he wants is for us to give him the glory, He wants us to give him the honor, the praise, the respect that he deserves because he is your daddy. You need to know that our heavenly Father is your daddy and you can talk to him. He loves us even more than you could ever imagine and He longs to be in fellowship and a relationship with you.

So friend, I want you to stop and think about everything in your life. Completely search your heart, and ask the Lord to search you and remove any darkness, hindrance, or anything that is holding you back from being exactly what the Lord has called you to be. The Lord needs you to stand tall.

Dry bones shall rise up to the name above all names, which is the name of Jesus Christ. Every person counts, and all of you are vital parts of the body of Christ. And every small move that you make is awesome because God is so proud of you. When you place God first, he honors you. He deserves every first in your life—the first part of your day, your first fruits. He deserves all that because your heavenly Father created you, friend. That is why we are to strive every day to be the image of Christ, to model Jesus, to be that image.

We thank you, heavenly Father for releasing divine wisdom to every person. We thank you, Lord, that you're covering us with the blood of Jesus. And as we step out in faith, we have a legion of heavenly angels going with us. So be obedient; whatever the Holy Ghost tells you to do, do it with due diligence and joy. We must come before God with thanksgiving, friends. Let's give him the honor, the praise, and the glory that he deserves. Let's get out there; let's tell our testimonies. Let's get people saved and never be ashamed to share the love of Jesus.

I have a quick testimony to share. I was at Sam's Club, getting a tire from my car, when I ran into a gentleman in a wheelchair. The Holy Ghost prompted me to go talk to him. I went over and talked to him. Guess what? He was very depressed. It was a divine appointment. The Lord used me to help him reconnect to his Savior. See how important it is to listen to the Holy Ghost? So when the Holy Ghost tells you to talk to someone, you do it because you just may be, as I've always told you, "The only Bible that some people may ever read."

So get out there. Be grateful for everything the Lord has done for you. Carry an attitude of praise and worship all day long. Remember to always honor the heavenly Father and the divine people God places in your life. We should exalt the name of Jesus Christ. We should thank the Lord God for everything that he is doing in our lives.

We give you praise, honor, and glory. Thank you, Jesus. Thank you, Lord. Father, we thank you for everything that you're doing, we thank you for your mercy and your amazing grace. We give you the praise, the honor, and the glory that you so deserve.

Just remember the final weapon is what keeps you, and that's prayer. Prayer covers and clothes you like a mantle. The Bible declares we should pray always, with all prayer and supplication in the Spirit. And as infantry soldiers during basic military training, we must learn to assemble and operate our armored weapons, especially under the most stressful conditions. So whatever is going on in your life, get in the Bible and read it. If you don't understand it, get into a Bible study, and get on some good, anointed teachings with teachers who can help you. Ask the Holy Spirit to lead and guide you. The Holy Spirit is the greatest teacher you will ever have. So get out there, and be the champion God has created you to be. Share the love of Christ, and make sure that your home is a home of prayer. Pray over your home, your family, your ministry, and your business. We should constantly be in prayer for everyone across this great nation. And we should definitely be united in lifting up our president, leaders, pastors, teachers, and mentors. We should be consistent in thanksgiving, fasting, and praying for them.

Whenever you get the chance, always be ready to plant a seed to win lost souls and expect faith. God will open the windows of heaven and pour out a blessing for you that there shall not be room enough to receive, as in Malachi 3:10. So friend, I'm extending this opportunity for you to sow a seed with Joy Today Ministries.

If you hear the Lord telling you to help spread the gospel, go to joytodayministries.com and click donate. Watch the Lord bless your socks off.

Go out there, have a victorious day, and be the champion God created you to be. I decree and declare that you'll go from victory to victory, strength to strength, and glory to glory in the mighty name of Jesus Christ. God richly bless you.

5

Love

Prayer

We should be up rejoicing and thanking the Lord for another day. We are so blessed, and we need to give him the honor, the praise, and the glory that he deserves for he is so great. So how are you guys today? If you feel led to give or sow into this ministry, you may do so by going to joytodayministries.com and clicking donate. Every seed counts.

You're giving unto the Lord, and he honors that. Let's lift our hands to heaven. Let's magnify the name of Jesus together. Let's unite in one accord across this great nation. Let's pray:

> Heavenly gracious Father, we come to you today, thanking you for waking us up this morning, thanking you, Lord, for the blessings that you have bestowed upon us, thanking you for coffee, thanking you for electricity, water, gas at home, clothes on our back, wonderful divine friends, and the honor to be able to pray and worship and release your Word as you're releasing it from heaven. Amen.

Message

So friend, I couldn't hold this back. The Lord woke me up and said, "Go do this." So I got up. I'm not all the way ready, but it's okay because God understands. He told me to release this because there's somebody here today who needs to hear this word. It's important that you receive it in the name of Jesus and run with it. Okay, so we're going to talk about Luke chapter 9 if you have your Bibles go to Luke chapter 9.

The one who thinks no one completely understands their situation because it is so odd and weird, you know what? Your heavenly Father does understand your situation. No matter how you're hurting, no matter what's going on in your life, your heavenly Father totally understands.

I remember back when I was young in rural West Virginia. Every Sunday when I was a little girl, the most precious time that I had was going to church with my grandma. My grandma, such a wonderful woman of God. My grandfather Paul, my dad Leroy, and my family faithfully went to church every Sunday. Sometimes we walked up the hill to a little old country church. I remember when I was probably like four years old, we were all going up the hill to church. I was so excited because that was the key part of my day, going to church with my family, walking up that hill, happy, singing, rejoicing with my family, and going to church to serve the Lord. I had a Sunday school teacher who was the light of my day. He was so happy and loved teaching us kids. And that is what it's all about, friend. It's about having that love, it's about having that joy, it's about having that spring in your step. And when you go through hard things, you sometimes lose that smile and joy. You lose the will to get out of bed and go to church, to leave and take someone with you.

The Lord brought me here to teach his family—that is you—what it's like and remind you how important it is to have that smile, to do

36

that dance, to sing that song, to reach out to that one person who doesn't have anybody. You know, we all go through things in our lives, and sometimes we don't have a clue why they happen to us. But guess what? Sometimes God allows things to happen to us to teach us or to make us stronger, to make us better people. Then we can share that testimony with everyone else.

Most of us have gone through similar things. But I have a God who brought me through. I have a God who turned my mourning into dancing. We serve a God that turns our mourning into dancing. We serve a God that turns our messes into miracles.

When you're out there living in the world, going to parties, living it up, and doing all the things that you feel make you happy, you don't really grasp the concept of what it's like to have a relationship with your heavenly Father. Rather, you think you've got it all under control. You think you're making all the money you could possibly make. You're driving that car, living in that house, living it up. You've got that babe you've always wanted, but something just doesn't feel right. Does that touch you, friend? Is that you? Are you that one person who thought you had it all? These are the ones who think they have it all because they've got five million dollars in the bank, driving the most expensive car, and live on the yacht. But if you don't have a relationship with your heavenly Father, you don't have anything because those are materialistic things, and they will all fade away. But that love for the Father surpasses all understanding—that love that is there when nobody else is there; that love that is there when your hair turns gray, and you're just not as perfect as you used to be when younger; the love that comes only from the relationship with your heavenly Father. That's what you need when you're looking for a relationship.

You need to understand that you have a heavenly Father who will love you more than anybody on this earth could even begin to love you. And that is what the Lord brought me here to let you know. Maybe you're driving that dirt bike that you've always wanted. Maybe you're mudding in that four-wheel drive truck and you're going out those back roads with that chick on your side and you feel like you're on fire. But let me tell you, if you don't have a relationship with your heavenly Father, you don't have it all. Man will let you down, but your heavenly Father will never let you down.

As a young teenager, I rode down those back roads with my boyfriend after church, going around and looking at the sights and the beauty. I thought I had the world by my side because I had the man of my dreams. Let me tell you it's wonderful to have those experiences. But if you don't have a relationship with your heavenly Father, you don't have it all. So the Lord woke me up early to here and let you know that Jesus is the best friend you can ever have. He will never leave you; he will never forsake you. And he will always be there for you. He is faithful and loves you. He loves you more than that girlfriend; he loves you more than that boyfriend. He loves you more than those tight-fitting jeans that make you feel all that.

Jesus is your everything, and he brought me here to let you know that hell is real. Hell is real. There's burning, there's gnashing of teeth, and there are demons. I don't even want to think about it. It's horrible.

The Lord brought me here this morning because he cares about you, friend. He cares about your spirituality. Men, he cares about you as the spiritual heads of your homes. You are the spiritual heads of your homes, women. You are wonderful warriors who step in the gate and help keep men in line. And let me tell you, we all have to join together in one accord for his glory, for his glory alone and not our glory. It's all for him.

I don't care if you're somebody who has dabbled in sin. Maybe you're cheating on your mate, maybe you've been going out to the bars, maybe you've been looking for all the answers in vodka. Or maybe you've been thinking, *Well if I get that wonderful woman who is so gorgeous, my life will be complete.*

Friend, your life is complete only when you let Jesus into your heart. When you let Jesus into your heart and establish a relationship with your heavenly Father, your life's complete. Then you start reading the Bible every day. Next you get rid of the toxic friends who keep saying, "Come on, let's go out to the bar. Let's go do this; let's go do that." Listen, they're still good people, but they're living in the world. They're not going to be there when times get difficult. What you need are real, godly friends who will be there for you through thick and thin. Ask yourself, "Who was there for me?" when you were going through all of life's tragedies. When you're going through all these rough times, who was there for you? Search your heart, friend. Today is your day to be set free. Today is your day to begin your life anew as in Jeremiah 29:11.

God wants to do a new thing in your life today. He wants to give you the best friend that you could ever have, one who will stick with you closer than a brother. And his name is Jesus. All you have to do is bow your head, or however you wish to do it, and cast all that care, all that worry, all that pain to him. It's all you have to do. It's a big thing because God wants to turn your life into a limitless life, a life of prosperity, a life of joy, a life of love. What's stopping you right now? Throw your hands in the air and say, "Father, I don't want to control everything. I surrender my life to you. I give myself to you; use me. If you can use this little country girl from the hills of West Virginia, then use me for your glory."

That's what it's all about, friend. It's about surrendering because we can't handle everything on our own. You can try every way that you can to be the best person that you can by yourself, but I'm going to tell you it's not going to work. One day your hair is going to turn gray; one day you're not going to be the same person you used to be in the flesh. But with Jesus, with God, all things are possible. And if you're out there looking for that lifelong mate, guess what? The lifelong mate is going to be the one who will love your heart. He or she is going to see your beautiful heart and how much love, real love, is in your heart because that's where real love comes from.

So I have a very important question to ask you friends. This is important because God got me out of bed this early this morning to make sure you have the opportunity to know that you have a friend who loves you more than oxygen, more than chocolate, more than football. And his name is Jesus Christ. For God so loved the world that He gave His only begotten Son so that you and I would never perish but have everlasting life.

If you were to die this very second, do you know without a shadow of a doubt that you would go to heaven? If you can say yes, that's great. If not, now is the time to surrender and say, "Dear heavenly Father, I need you in my life. Take over the reins of my life. Bring Jesus into my heart, wash me, cleanse me, fill me afresh and anew with the beautiful Holy Spirit." If you said that prayer, repented of your sins, and asked Jesus to come into your heart, welcome to the family of God. That is the greatest decision you could ever make because Jesus will stick with you closer than a brother.

When tragedies happen or things happen in life to you, brother, when we go through things that we don't want to go through, Jesus will be there for you when nobody else will. In order to establish a heavenly relationship with him, you must grab the Bible, open it, and actually read it. You can't leave it on the shelf to only pull out when life gets hard. You've got to read it on a day-to-day basis. You can't just leave it in the car for Sunday morning and then grab it when you're going into church. Guess what? If you do, you're only hurting yourself, your family, your wife, or your husband. It's that simple.

God gives us these instructions right in the Bible. We have the greatest gift that we can ever have, and that's the Bible. All the instructions are in there for everything we go through. But you and I are so stubborn that we try to do it our ways. Have you ever been the person who says, "I'm going to figure it out. I think this sounds good and looks good, so I'm just going to try it this way. This time I'm going to see how it goes. Just do it now)?

The Lord's giving you another chance, friend. Don't go to vodka for answers, don't go to pills for answers, don't go to sex for answers, don't go to porn for answers. Don't go out there and buy a $50,000 car for an answer. Instead, go to the Bible, get in your secret place, and seek the Lord with all your heart. He longs to give you your heart's desires. He really does. But first and foremost, you've got to surrender to your heavenly Father. You've got to develop a relationship with Him.

I went through a phase where I thought that with the perfect hair, the perfect clothes, and the perfect Mustang, everything was better. But guess what? No it wasn't. Without a relationship with your heavenly Father and Jesus in your heart, it doesn't matter. Life is but a vapor, friend. Today is your day to simply surrender and say, "Heavenly Father, I made some mistakes, and I acknowledge it. But I also acknowledge that you are my daddy. Wash me and cleanse me. Fill me afresh and anew with your beautiful Holy Spirit. Create in me a new heart of flesh, not a stone heart that makes one hateful."

I'm preaching to someone who needs to hear this message. Jesus loves you, and the answer is here in the Bible: "for God so loved the world that He gave His only begotten son so that you should not perish." He loves you so much that he allowed his son to die on the cross for you.

You matter, friend, and I know you're hurting. I know it's hard when you're battling with that flesh. You want to satisfy the flesh, but let me tell you, put the flesh down, and look to your heavenly Father and say, "Heavenly Father, I surrender to you. I don't understand everything, but I need your help, heavenly Father. Help me turn my mess into a miracle for your glory." Tell the Lord all your cares, tell him all the stuff that's going through your mind. Give it to the Lord, all those little things that you think nobody else cares about. Your heavenly Father does cares. Whether or not you like your hair, your heavenly Father cares. Whether or not you like your clothes, your heavenly Father cares. The heavenly Father even cares about the friends who are in your life and the house you live in. Your heavenly Father cares about everything.

Jesus is here, and He is reaching out His hand to you. He is saying, "Take my hand because I care." And all those moments when you thought you were doing what the Lord told you to do but maybe screwed up a little, your heavenly Father cares. What he cares about the most is that you had bold faith, stepped out, and tried. So if the other people don't care, that's okay. Release it to the Lord, listen to the Lord, and do what the Lord tells you with joy. When you do that, angels are dispatched to help you.

Hell is real, and God does not want anyone going to hell. He wants all his precious family coming home to heaven with him when it's your time. But right now, he wants to get you straightened up, focusing on him, and getting your life in order. To do that, you have to surrender. You simply have to say, "I've made some mistakes in my life, Lord, and I'm sorry. I'm here to repent and ask for your forgiveness. I'm here to say I messed up. I tried to do it my way, but my way wasn't the right way." Surrender unto God and say, "Dear heavenly Father, I acknowledge that you sent your only Son, Jesus, to the cross. Wash me and cleanse me. Fill me afresh and anew with your beautiful Holy Spirit. Bring Jesus into my heart. Jesus, consume me. Holy Spirit, consume me and turn my life around." If you said that prayer, friend, welcome to the family of God. That is the greatest decision that you could ever make.

Now let's go to the Luke chapter 9. If you have a Bible, get it out. I want you to say, "I am what this Bible says I am, and I will do what the Bible tells me to do with joy and due diligence."

Let's start off with Luke 9:39: "And, lo, a spirit taketh him, and he suddenly crieth out; and it teareth him that he foameth again, and bruising him hardly departeth from him." And we continue:

> And I besought thy disciples to cast him out; and they could not.
>
> And Jesus answering said, O faithless and perverse generation, how long shall I be with you, and suffer you? Bring thy son hither.
>
> And as he was yet a coming, the devil threw him down, and tare him. And Jesus rebuked the unclean spirit, and healed the child, and delivered him again to his father.
>
> And they were all amazed at the mighty power of God. But while they wondered every one at all things which Jesus did, he said unto his disciples,
>
> Let these sayings sink down into your ears: for the Son of man shall be delivered into the hands of men.

But they understood not this saying, and it was hid from them, that they perceived it not: and they feared to ask him of that saying.

Then there arose a reasoning among them, which of them should be greatest.

And Jesus, perceiving the thought of their heart, took a child, and set him by him,

And said unto them, Whosoever shall receive this child in my name receiveth me: and whosoever shall receive me receiveth him that sent me: for he that is least among you all, the same shall be great.

And John answered and said, Master, we saw one casting out devils in thy name; and we forbad him, because he followeth not with us.

And Jesus said unto him, Forbid him not: for he that is not against us is for us. (Luke 9:40–50)

The Lord is for you, friend. The Lord has great things for all of you this morning. He wants to take all those unclean spirits out of you, the ones that are holding you back from being everything that he has created you to be. And it begins by simply surrendering your life to him and admitting that you made some mistakes. And we all have made mistakes.

The main thing is that we need to remain teachable. I don't care if you have a PhD in every subject. I don't care if you've read your Bible twenty thousand times. You must remain teachable every time you open your Bible. There's always something new to learn, and that's why it's so important that we renew our minds daily with the washing of the Word and that we worship daily with everything in us, like David. When you don't know what to do, throw those hands in the air and dance, sing, and worship your Lord. For if you can go out there and cheer for football or for that race car, and you can dance for whomever, then you most certainly can dance for your King, your Savior, your Father, your Daddy.

Look at what he has done for you. He created you in your mother's womb and longs to fellowship with you. He longs to have a relationship with you, and it begins by surrendering unto Him and saying, "Not my will but your will, heavenly Father. Not my way but your way, Lord. I trust you, Lord, because you created me, and you know what's best for me." So it's time to quit with double-mindedness. It's time to quit thinking that you're not valuable because you are valuable; all of you are diamonds. You're not a lump of coal; you're not all optical. You're really not, even though you may act like it. Glory to God. Hallelujah.

The Lord brought me here to tell you that you matter, so stop the stinking thinking, stop second-guessing yourself, stop being double-minded, stop wallowing in self-pity, and stop dabbling in sand. Start rejoicing and worshipping. And get in that Bible and read it.

Do we believe 100 percent that the Lord has us? Do we believe 100 percent that the Lord gives the best life we could ever have if we believed in him? It's right there in his Word. Believe it and receive it. What does the word "believe" mean? To be firm, stable, established, and persuaded so solidly in His causative form. Amen means to believe.

The Lord wants you to be established in him, so be established in the Lord. Not on alcohol, not on pills, not in materialistic things, and not in another human being. Be established in the Lord, and you will be established. Faith is the most famous derivative. Amen also conveys this idea.

May we have a victorious day. Go grab someone and go to church expecting the supernatural power of God. Go expecting a miracle today. Rejoice for the Lord loves you so much. Again, he brought me here this early to tell you that you matter. I don't care what your problem is, he is here to fix it. Take his hand, and let him into your heart. Let him clean you up, and then let him bring divine people into your life as well.

If you don't ask, you'll never receive. And if you don't open that door, it'll never open. If you don't close that bad door, it'll never close. It's up to you, friend. You have free will. Do you want to keep the stinking thinking? Do you want to keep wallowing in self-pity and doing the things you know are not getting you anywhere? Or do you want to stand tall, grab that Bible, and say, "As for me and my house, we're going to serve the Lord, and we're going to serve him with gladness and with joy." Let that be your song today, all your life.

The Lord has been faithful even when I messed up, even when I made the wrong decision, and even when I went my way for a little while. My heavenly father has been faithful, and he will be faithful to you, too, if you open your heart and let Him in. Will you open your heart today, friend? Will you open your heart and let Jesus all the way in. Just say, "Forgive me for my sins. Cleanse me; fill me afresh and anew with your Holy Spirit." Try it. Try Jesus. Try the Bible. He'll never fail you. He will never forsake you, and he's here to turn your life into one of limitless love that only comes from heaven. Life is truly but a vapor, and you are truly his precious sons and daughters. It is time to arise. It is time to truly live, to truly love, to truly laugh, and to truly enjoy life.

How do you do that? First and foremost you've got to accept Jesus into your heart. You've got to start reading your Bible. And you've got to choose better friends. Bring the friends to church with you. Let's get each other saved because everyone matters. I don't care who you are, you matter. I don't care where you've been, you matter. I don't care what you've done, you matter. The Lord needs you to be the voice. The world needs you. I want you to be the voice that the world needs. Simply surrender it all to him, and ask Jesus into your heart. Make this the day of new beginnings (Jeremiah 29:11). The Lord wants to do a new thing, but you have to stop the stinking thinking. You have to quit the barhopping and popping pills in search of the answers. You've got to turn to him. You've got to turn to your heavenly Father for he wishes to turn that situation that's been worrying you so much. Maybe you made some mistakes and are feeling guilty. The Lord wants to turn that mess into a miracle. Let it go. Release it right now to him, and ask Jesus to come in, wash you, cleanse you, and fill you with the Holy Spirit. Let him do it. Try it. You've got to surrender to God.

He loves you more than anything, He created you, and he wants you to be happy. He wants to see you happy, smiling, dancing, and rejoicing with people.

If there's anything you need to change, anything that needs to be purged, just release it to your heavenly Father. Repeat this prayer aloud:

> Dear heavenly Father, I made a mess of my life. I surrender to you. Your will, not my will be done. Forgive me for messing up; forgive me for trying to do everything my way, dear Lord.

Heavenly Father, bring Jesus into my heart. Wash me, cleanse me, and fill me afresh and anew with your beautiful Holy Spirit. I acknowledge that you sent your only Son, Jesus, to the cross, and I thank you Lord that you love me in spite of myself.

If you said that prayer, welcome to the family of God. Now go out and spread that love to everyone you possibly can. Get somebody to church. The main thing is to read your Bible so that you know and you're equipped. If you don't read it, you're not going to know what the

Lord has to say. So read your Bible aloud to your family, pray with your family, actually talk with them eyeball-to-eyeball, worship with them, and have fun. Make this a wonderful day. Jesus loves you. He loves you so much. You are blessed and highly favored. I bless you. I bless your family. I bless your business. I bless your ministry. I bless everything that you put your hands to. Everywhere you go, you're taking territory for the Lord. You are now going from victory to victory, strength to strength, and glory to glory. Your past does not define you because your past is gone once you confess and release it to your heavenly Father. It's covered under the blood; let it go. Your past should never be brought up again.

Rejoice and go on. Step out of that, and be the wonderful person that God has created you to be. God richly blesses you. Go out there and find five people to give a love hug to. Let them know that they matter. Share a cup of coffee or tea or maybe a glass of water with them. Get out there, get some exercise, and get yourself in the best shape that you can be because God is getting ready to use you. God is getting ready to use you for his glory. And remember, your body is not yours, it belongs to the Lord. So you need to keep the Lord's body and shape healthy and clean.

If you feel led to sow into this ministry, please do so now by going to joytodyaministries.com and clicking donate. Your seed counts, and when you sow your seeds, believe that you're going to receive God's blessings. You are blessed and highly favored. You're blessed coming in, and you're blessed going out. Have a victorious day.

6

Obedience

Prayer

Let us join together in prayer and supplication: "Dear heavenly Father, we humbly come before the throne of grace, lifting up our Holy hands to heaven, saying, 'Holy, Holy, Holy is the Lord God Almighty.'"

I was in the middle of my day when the Holy Ghost stopped me and said, "I want you to go on and give this word of prayer and encouragement." If you're the one this word is meant for, then God bless you. God richly blesses each and every one of you. Let us start off with prayer:

> Heavenly Father, we come united in one accord for your glory across this nation, lifting our holy hands to heaven and saying, "Holy, Holy, Holy is the Lord God Almighty." We've come to worship you. We've come to give you the honor, the glory, and the praise that you so deserve. Heavenly Father, we thank you for each and every person who has touched this broadcast and replay. We thank you, Lord, for the power of your work.

We thank you, Lord, for the power of prayer. We thank you, Lord, for the honor to be able to preach, to teach, and to pray. Father God, we thank you that you're an action God, that you're on time, and that you're a faithful God. For the word that God speaks is alive and full of power, making it active, operative, energizing, and effective. Amen.

Message

So friends, I have come here to tell you how important it is to be obedient. As I was praying, worshipping, and spending time in a quiet place today, the Lord told me he wants me to reiterate to his family out there how important it is to be obedient.

The level of your obedience is so important it's a matter of life and death. So if the Holy Ghost tells you to do something, you must do it diligently with joy in your heart and thanksgiving that God has released that instruction and to you the power of action.

We have to obey that word. We have to speak that word over our circumstances with joy and thanksgiving and with boldness. God bless you guys. The power of obedience and action go hand-in-hand, friends. So I want you to understand that the level of your obedience determines so much in your life. It's up to you, friend.

The Lord is extending his hand to you today. He brought me here to tell you how much he loves you and how much he adores you right where you are. No matter what's going on in your life, no matter what the circumstances are, your heavenly Father totally adores you.

The past few days my phone has blown up with calls from people with domestic situations, addiction problems, and relationship problems.

And yesterday afternoon, my heart was so hurting because I have such a passion to want to help people. I was at a point in a place in my life where I felt that I had nothing and no one.

I remember crying out to God. I remember crying out to him with everything in me. I said, "Father, I want to do it right this time. Please guide me to the right people to help me do it right this time." I felt that I had made so many wrong choices, including attracting the wrong people. I felt like nothing was going right, and I was hurting. I was broken and looking for answers.

I got in my vehicle and headed up the interstate, I had praise and worship music on my radio. I was praying through the tears, "Lord, I'm sorry if I screwed up. I'm sorry if I made the wrong choices, but God I want to get it right this time. I really want to get it right this time. I have my family that needs me, and I want to make a difference." And you know, that night as I was traveling on that interstate, I came out to this bend in the road. I had my cruise on and my praise and worship on. And I was just crying with everything. Mainly because I didn't understand why all these negative things were happening to me. I reached out to God, "Father, I need your help," I said to him in a way that I had not reached out to him in a while. You know, sometimes in life we get so into ourselves that we don't realize we're going the wrong way.

And that night, I came around the bend, and there was a vehicle sitting along the road. I quickly slammed on my brakes with everything in me. And at that moment, my SUV went rolled three times and landed on its top. I was hanging by my neck. As I hit hard, I said to God, "Father, whatever I've done, I ask for your forgiveness, and I want to get it right this time. Please help me. Please. Don't let me die. I have a family that needs me." At that second, it was like angels appeared in that SUV. I felt the glory of God, and I knew I was okay. Even though the vehicle was upside down, every window was shattered, and I was this far from the windshield with the glass all over me, I felt the presence of the Lord. I had a peace that surpasses all understanding. I didn't understand what was going on, but I knew that God had answered my prayer. I knew no matter what, I was going to be okay.

At that moment that evening, five or six wrecks t happened at the same time. So there was a late response from people coming to help me, so I just began praying with everything in me. "Father, send me help. I thank you for sending me help."

A person in a big black Dodge drove onto the median right beside me. Out came this really tall bald man. He came over to the side of my SUV and asked, "Are you okay?"

Looking from the side, my vehicle must have looked like a Transformer if you saw it. You would have thought that I wouldn't be alive. All I could say at that particular moment was, "I'm okay. You know, I'm okay. The seat belt saved my life."

As a result of the accident, I completely rededicated my life to the Lord. I told him, "I will do whatever it takes, Lord, for your glory." It was at that particular moment in time the Lord showed me that I was valuable, that my life was valuable, that I mattered, and that sometimes we go through things we don't fully understand. But God understands. And even though you may feel like nobody cares, you have a heavenly Father who loves you more than anything.

All I could think about were my kids and my family. I was able to get hold of my oldest son. He came, and nothing was going to stop him from getting to me and letting me know how much he loved me as a friend.

I'm here today to tell you hell is real. God brought me here to let you know that the level of your obedience determines so much, and your testimony can save millions. It doesn't make any difference who you are, where you're at, what you have, or what you look like, you matter. You could have purple hair, gold hair, or no hair, your heavenly Father adores you just the way you are. And single men and women, if you think you have to turn yourself into someone you're not to attract the right mate, you're wrong. If God sends this person to you, that person is going to love you from their heart. That person is going to love you for who you are and what you stand for. It's not going to be because maybe you're twenty pounds overweight, and he or she thinks you're not good enough. Let me tell you, God says you're good enough. And today the Lord brought me here to tell you that you matter.

If you've never asked Jesus to come into your heart, today is the day because Jesus wants your whole heart. He wants to turn your mess into a miracle, just the way that he turned my mess into a miracle. I'm glorifying God because my oldest son is doing so wonderfully. He's teaching Bible study, he's praising the Lord, he's going forward in his life. And Jesus wants to do that for you. I'm thankful for all my children, even my spiritual children clear across the world. I praise God. There is nothing that God will not do to help each and every one of you go forward in your life if you will but surrender yourselves unto him. "For the eyes of the Lord move to and fro throughout the Earth that He may strongly support those whose heart is completely His" (2 Chronicles 16:9). The Lord loves you just the way you are.

The power of your words frame your life, friend. So I decree and declare that you're all beautiful just the way you are. I want you to know you're beautiful, and it doesn't make any difference what anybody else thinks or says. Your heavenly Father is the only person who really matters. And yes, you want to get your life together. Yes, you want to be healthy. We are instructed in the Word of God to be healthy and take care of ourselves because we are not our own; we belong to the heavenly Father.

What I am trying to say is come as you are. There's room at the cross for you, friend. Jesus says come as you are, and give him your whole heart, all those burdens, all those worries, and all those anxieties that you float around in your head. Let's get rid of the double-mindedness today. Let's put on the full armor of God and be what God has created us to be. Hallelujah!

The power of action is amazing. When you act on what your soul believes, it attracts according to the action. For example, what you sow you reap. This is so true. If you sow kindness, if you sow love, if you sow compassion, those are what you're going to reap. If you go out of your way to help others, you're going to reap that. If you go out of your way to bless others, you're going to reap that. But sometimes we are misunderstood.

People have been reaching out to me here lately. Many reach out through texting. It can be so hard to understand what someone is trying to say through a text message. Sometimes you have to pull over and call the person and say, "What are you trying to say to me, friend, because texting can be so misleading, and then people are mad and upset because I don't understand the message?"

So clear communication is essential. That's why he wants you and I to get back to the basics and understand that hell is real. And you don't want to go there because there's no turning back. That's why he brought me here, brothers and sisters, to reiterate that to you. I'm not going to beat around the bush. I'm simply going to tell you that hell is real, heaven is real, Jesus loves you, and now's the time to surrender it all to your heavenly Father and say, "Father, I made a mistake of my life. I need your help. Please lead and guide me."

The hardest thing that people seem to have is loosing full control to the heavenly Father. We have to yield; we have to heal. You must give up control to your heavenly Father. You have to remember that your heavenly Father and Daddy loves you more than anybody could possibly love you. Your actions are so important. If God tells you to go someplace and you don't go, you may wonder why you're feeling depressed. It could be because you're not being obedient. The Lord has a reason for telling you to pick up and go to wherever He is telling you to go. It could be because he wants to use you in a big way. That's why it's so important that we listen to the voice of the Lord. Your actions are so important because there are many people who need to hear your testimony. Your testimony really matters.

Let's say, for example, I decided to apply for a job. I pray and dream about it. I believe that I will be chosen for it, and I decree with words that it will be mine. But if I do not act on the desire by submitting my résumé and taking that next step of faith, there's no connection for God's law of attraction to release the fulfillment.

What do I mean? You pray, and God tells you what to do. And if you don't take action, do what God told you to do, you have voided your miracle. And that's why the Lord brought me here to tell you that the level of your obedience determines everything in your life. God wants to use you, friend, but you've got to be joyfully obedient and serve with happiness. Sometimes you have to praise him through it. I know it's hard sometimes. It's really hard to fight through anxiety because you're wondering, *Did I really hear the Lord?* Let me tell you, you did hear the Lord, and it's important that you are obedient.

The mouth speaks what is in the heart. When your soul is aligned with God's truth, the mouth will speak life-giving words that create your world. So I decree and declare from this moment forward, friend, you're going forward. I thank you, Father, for releasing accountability partners to everyone out there to help them truly go forward.

Someone I was talking with the other day said, "You know, my family doesn't get me. My family thinks I'm strange," to which I replied,

"Well, you know what? When you get saved and ask the Holy Spirit to come into your heart, you will have a whole new big family. There's a scripture that talks to you about family. It tells you how your Christian family sometimes will be your family, and they'll be closer to you than your biological family because your family may not understand what God is doing in your life." That's okay because, friend, we have to remain single-minded. We have to obey the voice of the Lord.

We have to stand tall for Jesus because as we do that, Jesus will stand tall for us. If we completely submit ourselves to our heavenly Father and are the yielded vessels that he desires to use, then he is going to bring all that other stuff into alignment, and that's where it goes.

The level of your obedience determines the depth of the miracle he can flow in through you. Don't let anyone keep you from doing what the Holy Ghost tells you to do. If he tells you to do it, do it diligently. Do it with your whole heart. That's why when we surrender our lives to our heavenly Father, we want to give him our whole hearts, not just part of our hearts but our whole hearts. Jesus is saying today, friend, "That little bit of discomfort, release it unto me. Let me make you free." Remember when Jesus died on that cross, He died for you and me to be free of all sins. And he is activating you today, bringing you into alignment to do what he wants you to do, fulfilling your purpose.

In case no one has told you today, friend, you're beautiful. Jesus loves you; you're very important to the body of Christ. You're very important to your heavenly Father. He adores you. Hallelujah. Make it intentional to read the Word of God every day. Make it intentional to reach out to that person God's telling you to reach out to, and you know what? Your life matters.

I'm sending a virtual hug to you out there to let you know that you have brothers and sisters in Christ who love you, pray for you, and care for you. All you have to do is reach out. I had a situation yesterday, as

I was saying, when a certain somebody reached out to me. She was in a domestic violence situation, a very bad domestic violence situation. I began praying. Brothers and sisters, it's so important that when we unite in prayer for situations like this, we have to believe 100 percent that when we pray, God hears our prayers and releases the answers to our prayers. Hallelujah.

Out of your mouth comes the abundance of what is in your heart. So if you have fear, fear's going to come out. That's why you want to get rid of all fear, all negative thoughts, all stinking thinking in the name of Jesus. The mouth speaks what is in the heart. When your soul is in agreement and alignment with God's truth, the mouth will speak life-giving words and create your world. Your environment can mold and transform you, or you can mold and transform your environment. It all begins with your choice—your choice to ask Jesus into your heart or your choice to receive what the Lord is trying to do in your life. I thank you, Father, for releasing a heaven-like atmosphere to each and every person out there. I thank you Lord for releasing a refreshing of your Holy Spirit presence to each and every person out there. Hallelujah.

I choose to believe that God wants to create a new atmosphere for the entire nation, and it begins with you and I doing what we were called to do. Hallelujah. Thank you, Lord Jesus. God has put a dream in each of us, and it's up to you and I to dream bigger and to let our dreams act in the name of Jesus. Hallelujah.

Take time to dream, friend. Intentionally carve out some time to ponder and define the desires of your heart. It helps to have your pad and pen ready to write the words, to write the instructions. Remember that to help you define your dreams, you need to ask yourself, "What would I love to do if I had all the resources and people I needed and absolutely no limitations?" I would like to see fulfilment in each of my dreams. Make a list of the specifics. "What would my life look like if my dreams were fulfilled?" "What benefits would come into my life and the lives of others if my dreams were fulfilled?"

As you continue dreaming, take note of your emotions. What emotions are you feeling right now? Are you feeling joy? Are you feeling expectant? Are you feeling boldface? Are you feeling overwhelmed, doubtful, or fearful? If your emotions are negative, ask yourself why. God's law of attraction responds to your emotions, so you want them to be positive. God is full of joy, expectations of faith, and attraction. When you have that joy, faith, the joy of the Holy Ghost inside you, you attract all of that.

And that is what I pray over all of you today. As we unite in prayer, let's stop the negative thinking. Let's put on the full armor of God because remember, we're to be the image of Christ.

Again, remember the level of your obedience determines so much. God is often not going to give you the whole picture. He's going to give you a set of faith and joy because you matter. And for God to give you that type of instructions, he is going to use you in a big way for his glory. Hallelujah.

Here are some scripture references I want you to read:

> Genesis 12:2
> Deuteronomy 1:11; 8:18; 28:1, 2; 11:12
> 1 Kings 17:9–16
> 2 Kings 1:7
> Psalm 41:1; 84:11; 112:1, 9
> Proverbs 28:27
> Malachi 3:8–12

We need to get in our Bibles even more than what we currently are because you develop your relationship and identity in Christ the more time you spend in His Word, in prayer, and in worship.

Hallelujah, hallelujah, hallelujah. You have to trust the Lord 100 percent. I know when you're going through things it's hard to completely trust, but you have to trust your heavenly Father. He created you and will neither ever leave you nor forsake you because he knows what's best for you.

I know we have gone through several things, but the Lord wants you to know that he loves you, He adores you, and there is nobody else.

Your testimony matters. Just when you think your whole life has gone to shambles, God is actually doing something new. You need to believe and dream big because God is a big God. He longs to see you smile and be happy. He longs to see you out there doing what he created you to do. So I decree and I declare from this moment that there's no more stinking thinking. There's no more second-guessing yourself. There's no more belittling or self-sabotaging yourself. And there is no more running from the Lord. It's time for you to put Jesus first, to focus on Jesus. Take out those Bibles and study together. Read the Word of God aloud to each another. Pray together and worship together. Get out there and be with the Lord. Don't let anything stop you because you matter. Read the Word of God, decree the Word of God, and speak the Word of God.

Pray in the Holy Ghost. Listen to the Holy Ghost. Be obedient and do what he tells you to do. Even if you don't understand the instructions, do what he tells you to do because, as you take steps forward, he will release all the help that you need to go to the next chapter of your life. He just needs you to step out in faith and know that he has you. He needs you to have bold faith. So I decree and declare today, friend, that you are going forward. I decree and declare the heavenly Father is releasing accountability partners to all of you to help you go forward. I understand that sometimes you need someone to take you by the hand, pull you out of the ditch, and say, "Let's go this way." And that's okay.

I rebuke and curse mental illness. I curse all addictive spirits, Lord. I rebuke it. I curse it in the name of Jesus Christ, and I thank you, Lord, for releasing a sound mind in each and every person out there. I thank you, Lord, for releasing an impartation of bold faith to help them walk through it. I thank you, Lord, that you are opening the windows of heaven, and you're releasing a fresh anointing upon each and every person to do what you created them to do, go where you've told them to go, and be what you created them to be. And I thank you, Lord, that you are speaking to every heart out there right now, and that they are searching their hearts, and if they need to rededicate their life, they're rededicating their lives unto you. They're yielding unto you, precious heavenly Father, and they know they are to follow you and not man. You bow to nobody but your heavenly Father, friend.

Hallelujah. God richly bless each and every one. Visit joytodayministries.com and click donate.

God bless your soul.

7

Prayers

Prayer

Let us join together in prayer.

Dear gracious heavenly Father, we've come to worship you, we've come to honor you, we've come to lift our holy hands to heaven and give you the praise, the honor, and the glory that you so deserve. Precious heavenly Father, we honor, and we love you. We worship you; we say thank you for everything that you're doing for us. Holy Spirit, you are so welcome here.

Come saturate this broadcast and everyone at home. Saturate them with your love, your peace, your joy in the name of Jesus. We give you praise and honor; we give you glory for the lives you're touching and transforming in the mighty name of Jesus. Hallelujah. Thank you, Lord Jesus. Thank you, Lord, for your unrelenting love. You know, friend, your heavenly Father adores you. There is no one like you. Thank you, Lord Jesus.

Message

When you desire God as you desire the air that you breathe, you will find Him. When Jesus becomes your everything, you will find him. Doors will open; unending doors will open. Hallelujah.

Love is the highest and the most powerful law of God's kingdom. So when you release that love to your heavenly Father and love him with everything in you, he will shower you with the same love. He loves you so much that he brought me here to tell you that he loves you. His unconditional love made him to die on the cross for your sins. You must truly repent because the Lord will never leave you. If you truly repent of your sins and ask him to wash and cleanse you and fill you with a fresh anointing, you will receive miracles.

He loves you, friend. Sing praises to his name. Sing praises to your heavenly Father. Sing praises with understanding. Bless him. Sing praises to His name. God reigns over the nations. God sits on his holy throne. The promises of the people of God has gathered together. Everything goes away. The chains, worries, and anxieties drops from your life.

He is known as the refuge. For behold the kings assembled. They passed by together, they saw it, and so they marveled and were troubled. They hastened away with fear, which took hold of them, and were pained like a woman giving birth.

And when you break the ships, it tarnishes with an east wind as we have heard, so we have seen in the city.

According to your name, oh God, so is your praise to the ends of the earth. We should be praising him, friend. We should be praising our heavenly Father day and night for everything he has done, how far he has brought us in life, for what he is doing for us now, and for all the things that he is doing that we don't even know about. Great is our

God, and he's so worthy to be praised. Let the daughters of Zion be glad because of your judgments' work in Judah. Well, with her Borges, consider his palaces that you may tell it to the generation following that this is our God, and he will forever be our guide even to death. So when you mess up, simply repent and ask for forgiveness. Let it go for it's washed under the blood. The main thing is to focus on your relationship with Jesus. Going forward, don't make the same mistake twenty thousand times like a sheep.

Psalm 49:14–16 says, the upright shall have dominion over them in the morning. But God will redeem my soul from the power of the grave: for He shall receive me. Selah.

So you have triumphed by the power of asking Jesus to come into your heart and the Holy Spirit. Don't let stinking thinking take your blessings away, friend. The power of praise, the power of his love, the power of a steady mind are all in his Word. So it's time for us to rise up and be the godly Christian men and women he has created us to be. And he is doing a new thing as in Jeremiah 29:11. And he is releasing forgiveness, peace, and joy.

In the name of Jesus, thank you, Lord, for your mercy. Thank you for your amazing grace, and thank you for everything that you're doing.

You want to bear another's burdens? Then you need to fulfill the law of Christ (Galatians 6:2). If there are people who always seem to turn to you to solve their problems—such as your child, a spouse, a friend, a coworker, or even a parent—and you meet their needs, ask yourself, "Am I helping, or am I able to restore that person? My rescuing that person, am I trying to fix them? Am I needed by them? Am I standing in the way of what the Lord wants to do in their lives?" That's what I want you to ask yourself, friend.

There's somebody here today who needs to hear this word. When it comes to helping others, the Bible gives us clear instructions, such as when Apostle Paul says every man shall bear his own burdens (Galatians 6:5). It means that you have your own knapsack, and you are to set healthy boundaries as to what you get to put in it. You are responsible for not putting more in your knapsack than you can carry. Sometimes we try to help people who have not been taking good care of themselves. The Lord brought me here to tell you today that it's your day to realize that sometimes you have to release some things to other people and the heavenly Father because the Lord wants you to take care of yourself. You must not allow people to dump their issues on you and make you feel responsible for carrying them. It's okay to be a great listener. It's okay to pray for people. But again, you must not allow people to dump their issues on you. We're not meant to carry others' issues. We are meant to worship him. Allowing that enables that person to perpetuate your behavior; the behavior tolerated is a pig behavior.

When Paul says we are to bear each others' burdens, it's a different word. It means that when life gets too heavy for another person, you are to help that person lift their hands during that time.

God wants you to support others who are in need, but never to take on the responsibility of their lives, a person who is in perpetual need of you, a person who often puts more dependency on you than in God. There are times in life when people go through things and need their brothers and sisters. But first and foremost, we are to equip them and train them how to read their Bibles, how to get in their prayer closets, and how to go to God first. There's never anything wrong with reaching out to your brothers and sisters when you need help, but we are to teach each other and remind each other that we can equip ourselves better to handle these things if we first go to the Word of God. It's one thing to help a person with a legitimate financial need, tragedy, or sorrow, but it's another thing to bail someone out every time that he or she gets into a mess. You need to help that person to be a good steward. You need to help that person to begin to trust God to meet their needs because only God is always able to be there for that person. Sometimes you may not be there to answer that phone, you may not be there to pull them up out of the ditch, but God will always be there. Only God can meet all needs, friend. Only God is able to heal, restore, deliver, and bring a person to wholeness. You cannot be God to that individual, as much as you would like to.

There are some people here whose hearts I know are so kind and loving that if you could take your hands away for your friends, if you could take your hands away for your family, you would do it. But the best thing you can do as a friend is to pray, intercede, and encourage them. Get them in line with the proper counseling that can help them. You can sometimes take on too much, and then their burdens become yours, and their toxicities come into your peace. The goal is for us to minister as leaders of the gospel of Christ.

It's great to be able to say that we have divine friends in Christ who will minister to us and will fall to their knees. Praying for each other will, in fact, take action and help us become what God created us to be. You see, friends, sometimes you simply have to stand up and say, "No. I'm sorry, but I am extremely busy right now. Is it an emergency? Let's make an appointment, and I will get with you as soon as possible."

You cannot be God to everybody. You cannot be God to anybody. They have to develop their relationships with their heavenly Father so that they know when tragedy comes, they should first and foremost seek the throne.

Daddy never wants you to take on the role of the Holy Spirit or to be the end and be all for another person. Recognize that you can't be all things to all people. Friend, lifting someone out of a life-blowing situation is different than enabling someone and creating a codependency. So if you have a son or a daughter who's addicted to drugs, today the Lord brought me here to tell you not to enable your child. Don't slip your son or daughter twenty or thirty dollars because you're afraid if you don't, he or she might commit suicide. Don't do that. Pray for your child and get him or her the help needed.

The Bible never instructs us to turn all our problems over to another person. It doesn't. It instructs us to cast our cares upon the Lord. The truth is that God wants each of us to trust him 100 percent as the Source of our provisions, as the Source of our directions, as the Source of our healings, our way Maker and our Provider. He doesn't want us to depend anyone other than him for our purposes in life.

The readings to go along with that are John 13:34–35; Ephesians 4; Philippians 2:4; 1 Thessalonians 5:11; Hebrews 10:24; and James 2:14–17. So my prayer for you today, friend, is that we learn not to enable people but to equip them. We have to train them, we have to pray for them, we have to get them Bibles and study tools to help them become the people God has created them to be.

And yes, there are extenuating circumstances, friend. There are times and circumstances when we actually need to take someone's hand and pull him or her up and help another to walk through. I totally agree with that. But I hear strongly in my spirit the Lord is saying sometimes you have to release people unto Jesus, and pray for them silently. When the Lord says, "Go get that person. Go take them by the hand and help them," you must be obedient. That's why it's so important for us to first go to the throne. We go to God, pray, and ask the Lord, "How do I help my brothers and sisters to grow? How do I help my brothers and sisters get through the situation they're going in their lives?" And then we listen to the Holy Ghost, being obedient with joy. Because you see, when we do anything for the Lord, it is an honor and a privilege. So if the Holy Spirit is speaking to you, I am telling you to reach out. There's somebody going somewhere, and he's telling me to tell you to do it with joy, with thanksgiving, and with 100 percent trust. He needs you to trust him with all your heart today, friend.

If you have never known that you have a Savior and his name is Jesus Christ, if no one has ever told you about Jesus Christ, then let me tell you today you have a heavenly Father who loves you so much that he brought me here to say you have a friend, and his name is Jesus. He will stick with you closer than a brother. He will be there for you when no other person is. How do you discover that? By simply acknowledging that you have sinned and then repent from your sins. Kneel to your heavenly Father, and ask the Lord to forgive you and fill you afresh and renew you with the beautiful, precious Holy Spirit. And if you said that prayer, confess your sins to your heavenly Father, and ask the Lord for forgiveness. He has come to wash you and cleanse you. He has filled your freshman year with a beautiful Holy Spirit.

Welcome to the family of God. That is the greatest decision that you could ever make. God bless you, Lisa and Rick Nelson. God bless you, Moses. God bless you all. If you like and share the broadcast, others may receive this word, and that would be greatly appreciated because it's all about him. It's all about getting that word from heaven out to each and every one of you out there so they can be saved, healed, delivered, and whipped in on their way to their callings.

Heavenly father, I thank you for this divine service today. I thank you for the divine people you brought on here today, Father. I thank you that you are releasing healing balm to every person out there today. I thank you, Lord, that when we least expect it, that's when you release your Word to us that helped us in so many ways. We understand it. We know there are so many people who have hearts so big that they would love to personally save everyone across this great nation. Unfortunately, we can't do that. But through your power, internet, teachings, and uniting, we can all work together as a part of the family of God, the great army of God, to get it done.

Dear heavenly Father, I thank you right now that you're opening the floodgates of heaven and releasing heavenly warriors to go out there across this great nation to reach that one who maybe some of us didn't get. Father, I thank you that you consider everyone as precious as the other. I thank you that no one is to be left behind. Father, I thank you that you loved us so much that you sent your only Son, Jesus, to the cross.

As we go through the day, let us remember how much you truly love us that you send us divine people, divine teachers, divine mentors, divine pastors, divine evangelists, divine friends, and most of all, you sent us Jesus. What more could we ask for? We are so lucky. We are so blessed, friend, today once again.

So that's enough of the stinking thinking. That's enough of second-guessing yourself. That's enough of being poor always. You deserve to live a happy life. You deserve to live in that home you've always dreamed of. You deserve to hold someone you've always loved. The Lord is wanting to release that unto you now, friend. You just need to let him do it. Let him open the door and then walk through it. He says, "I've released the keys." The keys have been released to you, friend. It's time for you to take the keys out of those pockets. Put them in the door, open that door, and walk through it to go up the stairs and rejoice with your heavenly Father.

We're just taking you into the holy of holies today, friend. He's setting your feet in the holy of holies. Jesus is there with you, and he's saying, "Let Jesus hold you for a while, Let Jesus dance with you for a while. Let Jesus take away all your pains. Let Jesus take away all that sorrow." Let Jesus take away all those mistakes that you can't seem to let go of because you know what? Jesus cares, and he won't tell anybody.

Release those sins today, friend. Release them all to Jesus, and let Jesus wash you, let Jesus dance with you, let Jesus hold you, let Jesus be your best friend for this little moment. Let Jesus hold you in his arms.

This is so powerful. Someone needs to hear this. The anointing is here. Receive your healing today, friend. Don't you run from this message. Jesus loves you, and no matter what you have done, he is here to forgive you. He's stretching out his hand, and he is saying, "Come with me, friend, come with me. Let me in your whole heart. Let me dance with you. Let me hold you." You see, Jesus is the best friend you can ever have in the entire universe. He'll be there in the cool breeze of the day. He'll be there to sing with you and help you rejoice when you feel like you don't know how to rejoice anymore. He'll be there for you whenever something happens that you're not expecting to happen because Jesus loves you. Jesus loves you, and the Lord brought me here today to tell you that Jesus loves you more than you can ever imagine.

He longs for you to be totally set free from your past. Somebody is holding on to their past. Today is your day to walk out of that past. Step out of it right now in the name of Jesus. And I command the spirit of self-sabotage to flee from you now in the name of Jesus. There's no need to worry about the past, it is gone as in Jeremiah 29:11. God is doing a new thing for you this very second. From this moment forward, don't you look back because Jesus already paid that price. Remember, friend, when Jesus was on that cross, you and I were on his mind. And what did he say? He said, "Father, forgive them for they know not what they do."

Receive that in the name of Jesus. Receive your healing; receive your freedom. Be home in the name of Jesus Christ. Today is your day. Today is your day to rejoice, to sing, and to magnify the name above all names, to magnify the name of Jesus. Let us lift high the name of Jesus across this great nation. When we quit this stinking thinking and double-mindedness, and we praise him and read his Word, and we decree his words, he opens doors. Decree and declare it, and the Lord will bring it to pass. You can call him on his way.

You can bank on his Word. He will bring it to pass. Enough of the double-mindedness; it is gone in the name of Jesus Christ. You are healed, you are saved, you are on your way to the best days, the best months, the best years of your life. You deserve it, friend. You deserve it so much that your heavenly Father cared so much that he sent his only Son to the cross to die. Why? So you could be free of all the debris, free from the past, free from sin, free from darkness.

Remember Genesis 1 specifically tells you that in the beginning, God created the heaven and the earth, and the earth was without form. Void and darkness were upon the face of the deep. Then the spirit of God moved upon the face of the waters, and God said, "Let there be light." Friend, there was light. God saw that the light was good divided the light from the darkness. Let the darkness in your life go, and receive a light from heaven. Receive that heavenly sunlight that only heaven can give you in your life. Father God, I pray that you consume each and every person on this broadcast and repay with a heavenly light. Let your heavenly presence consume them with your Holy Spirit. Ignite them in the blessed and holy name of Jesus Christ.

> And God called the light day and the Darkness He called night and the evening and the morning were the first day and God said let there be a firmament in the midst of the waters and let it divide it from the waters. And God made the firmament and divided the waters which were under the firmament from the waters which were above the firmament and it was so and God called the firmament heaven.

And the evening and the morning were the second day and God said let the waters under the heaven be gathered together unto one place and let the dry land appear and it was so and God called the dry land Earth and the Gathering Together of the waters He called sea. And God saw that it was good.

God loves you, friend. We read that God is light, and God is love. Step into that light. Step out of the darkness that's holding you back, and allow him to consume you with the anointing that's coming through me to you in the name of Jesus. The Lord longs to hold you in his arms. The Lord longs to love you today. Just let Him into your heart. Let go of that past; let it go because it's already covered. Once you repent, it's gone. You don't have to confess it to fifty thousand people. Get on your knees or under that old oak tree or in your old truck.

And wherever you are—in your office, your airplane, your boat— confess that sin that's holding you back to your heavenly Father. Release it to your heavenly Father and let it go. Then worship him and thank him for his goodness. Thank him for his mercy. Thank him for his amazing grace because you see, Jesus loves you. He loves you so much, and he stretched out his arms. And once again, he said, "Father, forgive them for they know not what they do."

Today is your day. Receive that in the name of Jesus. Step out of that mockery clay and into your wonderful future that he has for you. I decree and declare that you're going victory to victory, strength to strength, glory to glory. I decree and declare that God is going to use you in a mighty way for his glory. I decree and declare divine open doors for you, friend. I decree and declare that from this moment forward, there will be no more stinking thinking. I decree and declare that this year is going to be the best year of your life. I decree and declare that you are going to the top of that mountain, and you're going to rejoice. You're going to make it because God's not done with you yet. I decree and declare that good thing God started in you, friend, he will finish because he loves you enough, and his Word says that he will finish what he started. Don't you ever give up.

There are so many people who need to hear your testimony. There are so many people who need to meet you. There are so many people who need to hear your story. So finish that book. Get it finished for God's glory. Finish what he is telling you to do. And remember, it's okay just to be you because there's only one you, and your story matters.

God richly bless each and every one of you. I am Melissa DeSerio with Joy Today's Ministries, letting you know that you have a Savior. His name is Jesus. He will never leave you. He will never forsake you, and he will never forget you.

Just remember Jesus loves you. Take his hand and walk the greatest life. Let him walk with you. Let Jesus talk with you. Invite Jesus into every conversation, into every relationship, into everything that you do. Watch your heavenly Father bless you; he will bless your socks off. I bless you to receive blessings. Father, I thank you for releasing blessing after blessing to everyone here today. And that the ones who listen to this on the replay, I bless you. I bless your families. I bless your ministries. You are richly blessed.

Until next time, get out there and share the love of Jesus. Share that testimony. Share that smile; turn that frown upside down. Quit second-guessing yourself. And when the enemy tries a twist, does it make you think weird things? Just shut up in the name of Jesus. Stand up, and start praising your Lord. Go forward for you are a chosen generation born to show his excellence. Go do it. Go be the champion God has created you to be. Love you guys. Bye for now.

8

Facing Your Challenges

Prayer

Coming on for some more prayer and encouragement. It's been like seven days since I've been with you all. So nice to see you again. As you're coming on, please like and share the broadcast.

Let's start off with prayer. Let's unite in prayer and supplication across the globe. Lift up your holy hands to heaven and say, "Holy is the Lord God Almighty."

> We thank you, kind and precious heavenly Father, for the honor and the opportunity to be able to unite in one accord across this great nation to lift up the holy name of Jesus. As you're coming on tonight, we're going to lift Jesus's name on high, thanking him for his goodness. We give our Father the praise, the honor, and the glory that he deserves. Holy is the Lord God Almighty.
>
> We've come to give you praise, precious heavenly Father. We have come to give you the respect because you're the owner and you deserve it.

So what I'm going to talk to you about this evening is a combination of a couple of little things the Lord has laid in my heart. And number one is he wants us all to move to higher ground tonight. So no matter what circumstance you're going through this evening, friend, he brought me here to tell you that tonight is your night to step up to higher ground, to be accelerated and go forth to your calling. So as you're hopping in place, like and share the broadcast. May God richly bless each and every one of you. Father, thank you for Holy Spirit discernment as I read your Word and I speak your words. I thank you, Lord God, that as I speak, it is your words that are being released through me from heaven to your family out there.

We're going to read Zechariah 2:10. We're talking about singing and rejoicing. If we're going through things friend, you and I must always sing and always rejoice through it. Sometimes when everything seems to be going crazy and hectic, we simply don't know what to do. But our heavenly Father just wants us to chill out, step out of the situation, and just worship him. Sing and rejoice and remember how far he's brought you, friend.

I have a quick but important question to ask you tonight. If you were to die this very second, do you know without a shadow of a doubt that you would go to heaven? If you can say yes, that is so wonderful. But if you're saying no or that you don't know, surely the Lord brought me here to tell you tonight is your night to be tenacious. Tonight I want you to stand tall, to say "yes" and "Amen" and to receive the Lord into your hearts.

You see, sometimes we don't know what to do. Sometimes we're faced with circumstances that we simply just don't know how to handle. I remember going through all kinds of things, and I received a lot of phone calls the past couple days from people needing prayer. That's why I decided to come on and do this all together, to pray for all of you at the same time, and let you know that my heart goes out to each and every one of you. I know there are all different situations going on out there, where you're faced with different things. I'm here to tell you that if you'll sing and rejoice, you can say your way through anything because with God, all things are possible. Not some things but all things are possible.

God bless you all. The past three days I had the honor of helping minister at a conference in Tulsa, Oklahoma. It was very exciting to see the power of the Lord and the Holy Ghost move in a mighty way. We're very thankful for that.

The scripture that I want to share with you is,

> Sing and Rejoice O Daughter of Zion for lo I come and I will dwell in the midst of thee and the Lord and many nations shall be joined to the Lord in that day and shall be my people and I will dwell in the midst of thee and thou shalt know that the Lord of hosts has sent me unto thee and the Lord shall inherit Judah his portion in the holy land and shall choose Jerusalem again. Be silent before the Lord be silent. Oh All Flesh.

The Lord is telling all of us to put our flesh down. For the Lord is raised up out of his holy habitation and showed me Joshua, the high priest, standing before the angel of the Lord, and Satan standing at his right hand to resist him. God rebukes Satan at verse 2: "And the Lord said unto Satan the Lord rebuke thee o Satan even the Lord that hath chosen Jerusalem rebuke thee. Is this not a brand put and plucked out of the fire."

You see, the Lord is wanting to pull some people out of the McCurry play clay tonight. He wants to pull you out of the fire and into his peace. So this evening, remember that whatever situation you may be facing, whatever it is that you may feel is too hard, the Lord brought me here to tell you that nothing is impossible with him. No matter what you're going through—even if you're going through relationship issues, if you've lost your job, if your spouse has left you, if you're having trouble with prodigal children—no matter what your situation is, there is no situation too bad that your heavenly Father cannot help you get through it. And out of the abundance of our mouths come joy and peace. And so tonight he wants us to unite and join in prayer for everyone across the great nation. He wants us to intercede for everyone across this great nation.

The name of Jesus. There is no way to heaven without Jesus. So friend, I'm here to tell you that Jesus will stick with you closer than a friend. And I feel the anointing very strong. He's here tonight. And no matter what circumstance you're facing, no matter what uncertainty you may be facing, Jesus is here. Simply surrender the whole situation, and let Him take your hand. He longs to hear your voice. He longs to come in and turn your situation around for you. But first you've got to surrender 100 percent of your life and problems to the Lord. I feel that so strongly.

There's somebody here who's having a very serious issue with a prodigal child. A prodigal child they have been praying for, and they're hurting really badly tonight. So friend, we're on air tonight, interceding for your brothers and sisters, and we are praying. We're praying and we're interceding and we're thanking the Lord for releasing divine help to you, whoever you are. You know who you are. It's okay if you're hurting right now because the Lord's coming into the situation, and he is smoothing it out. The Holy Spirit is not the author of confusion. The Holy Spirit is the author of peace, and we've come here tonight as your brothers and sisters in Christ to let you know first and foremost that we care about you. No matter how messed up your situation is.

No matter how odd somebody may think you are, your heavenly Father loves you and is opening doors for you that no man can shut. But the first thing you have to do is completely surrender the whole situation to him and simply say, "Dear heavenly Father. I need your help. I acknowledge that you sent Jesus Christ to the cross to die for me. Please come into my heart. Jesus, fill me afresh, and renew me with your precious Holy Spirit." If you said that prayer, my friend, welcome to the family of God. Asking Jesus to come into your heart and refresh you with the Holy Spirit is the greatest decision that you could ever make. You're now on a new journey. You're now going to a higher ground. Thank you, sister Carol, for playing higher.

That's what God wants to do for all of us. He wants us all to go to higher ground and to him. He's realigning and redefining our lives. He is moving us all to higher ground because he needs us to come into full alignment to do what he called us to do. You know, while I was praying, I heard him saying we're at a very important time of acceleration, friend. He needs you to be very obedient to his voice. You know, his Word says his sheep hear his voice. So listen very closely, and be obedient because the Lord needs you; the Lord needs your testimony. The harvest is ready, but the laborers are few. So let's sing and rejoice and thank him for his goodness. Let's thank him for what he has done, what he is going to do, and what he's doing behind the scenes that you and I didn't even realize. And remember that your life is the only Bible that some people may ever read.

This takes me to Matthew 13, about the fullness. We're talking about harvest; we're talking about revival. The net is full. The harvest is ready.

And he said, "Dry Bones rise up in the name of Jesus." Come in full alignment, march forward, and see everyone out. There's a very important part of the body of Christ, your heavenly father. He brought me here tonight to let you know that he wants you to go higher.

Focus on Jesus. Read his Word more. The more you grab your Bible and read the Word of God, the more you go deeper into him. When you know who you are in Christ and then you speak his Word over your circumstances, you'll watch the mountains fly away in your life. According to Mark 11:23, "You and I have the authority to command these mountains to move in our lives." Your case is different. You are victorious. You're an overcomer. You're blessed. You're highly favored. You're an ambassador of heaven. You're on your way to heaven, and there's no turning back. He just needs you to surrender that 100 percent that you keep holding back.

He wants me to tell you that you should love him more than anything else. More than your brother, than your spouse, your sister, he knows what's best for you. But he needs you to surrender. Whatever your problem is—whether you're having trouble with alcohol or painkillers—I hear that tonight's your night to be set free. Just release it all unto Jesus. Say, "Jesus; I need your help. I break off that addiction problem in the name of Jesus." And we command any wrong voice speaking to your head, telling you things, to go in the name of Jesus. Once you ask Jesus to come into your heart and receive the Holy Spirit, we ask the Holy Spirit to refresh you because you're born again. You're filled with afresh with the precious Holy Spirit. Read the Word, and shut out all those other voices. Listen to the Lord, and do what the Holy Ghost tells you to do. That's important. Do what the Holy Ghost is telling you to do because the level of your obedience affects so many people in these last days.

You know Peter is one of my favorites. He's a risk taker, he's got a temper, he's a street fighter, and he cuts off ears. He's rough on the edges, but Jesus never tries to polish him. I like that God surrounds himself with every type of personality. We have all types of personalities here, but it doesn't make any difference because God created you. He loves you the way you are. God wants to use us just the way we are, friend.

Peter was also a water-walker, which you need to read about in Matthew 14:22–33. When he saw Jesus walking on the water, Peter said, "I'm going for it." And Jesus wants you and I to go for it too. He wants you and I to go for our dreams, to go for what he's called us to do. Tonight step out. He didn't wait; he didn't hesitate. You see, when the Holy Ghost tells you to do something, if you wait, you will cause more problems. You're causing problems for yourself and your family when you're not obedient. Do what the Holy Ghost tells you to do.

This is getting deep because when the Holy Ghost tells you to step out, he's wanting to use you in a way that is very important. Sometimes the riskiest thing you will ever do is to always play it safe. Sometimes you have to go for it. When you start walking on water, it's called faith, friend. Bold faith. It's going to feel funny because your flesh will be screaming its alarms.

Then you often feel the criticism from other people setting in the boat. Whether they're saying it aloud or not, they now have to justify why they are still setting in the boat while you're walking on water. What a night! God wants all of you to walk on water. He wants you all to step in the calling he has placed in your lives.

Peter has the tenacity and enough faith to get out of the boat. He did something besides sit around and wait, wonder, and second-guess himself. You see, friend, that's why Jesus wants us to quit being double-minded. You see, if you've been saved and filled with the Holy Spirit, you're reading the Word, going to a Holy Ghost–filled church, and praying in your closet, you'll hear the Lord. So quit second-guessing yourself. You know what God told you to do, so do it.

Enjoy and don't let anybody else stop you from doing what the Lord told you to do, friend, because it doesn't make any difference what your circumstances are two years from now. When you turn your life over to the Lord and surrender unto him, you invite the Holy Spirit to come in and wash you and cleanse you. And ask the Holy Spirit to take the reins of your life. So you have to trust him; you have to step out. Remember that Peter was a tenacious person. He had bold faith, and that's what the Lord wants you and I to have. A very bold faith so that we get out of that boat for it.

So God brought me here tonight to tell you tonight's your night to get out of the boat, to not sit there and wonder when and how you should do this or do that. He wants you to get out of there and do the needful. Do something besides sit around and wait. He took only action, friend. I have often said you will only find success. I bind whatever is distracting you and confusing you right now in the name of Jesus.

Here's the principle: Falling down is not failure; staying down is failure. So when you fail, you miss it, and you sink. But you get out of the boat, and you take some steps, even if they're baby steps. Jesus is standing nearby to give his rescue. Hey, next time you might take some leaps instead of baby steps. Does it feel funny to your flesh? Yes. That's because you're moving in a different room than you've normally moved in. Faith is a spiritual realm. Are you always going to know every correct, safe step to take and have to water-walk a hundred times and with no faith? No. The Lord wants you and I to have bold faith because everything that we go through is a test. It's a test to see if we're going to stay, if we're going to truly step out, if we're going to truly do what the Lord is telling us to do. The Lord needs to see if he can count on you and me to be there when he needs us to be there, to teach when he needs us to teach, to give when we need to give, to receive when we need to receive, to help our brothers and sisters when they need help.

Mrs. Romy, I'm here to say don't you give up. You're not stupid, and there's room at the cross. For even you, friends. And no matter what you did, even if you have excellent trouble with alcohol, just don't be down. Jesus is here. Surrender that problem unto him, and receive your healing now in the name of Jesus. Your faith to sink is broken. Focus tonight; review whatever is breaking you, friend. We rely on you according to the Word of God. And we say, "Holy Spirit, take over our thoughts, take over our focus, lead us and guide us the way you want us to go in the name of Jesus."

So let your eyes look straight-ahead. Friend, you think it might be lonely on the water. Keep walking for his greatness awaits all of us. His greatness is waiting on you if you'll step out, stand tall, and hit the reset button. Take your sword, and march forward for the calling. That's what my word is. Just remember that falling down is not a failure; staying down is the failure. So when you fail, you missed it. But you got out of the boat and took some steps, right? So tonight, friend, the Lord wants you to get out of that boat. Even if you follow them down, even if you kind of parked your boat a little bit and are lying back and saying, "Lord, I don't know what to do tonight," friend, you do know what to do: Focus on Jesus. You pray, worship him, and go forward, trusting him. And you march forward.

There's an important part of the army of God, friend. The Lord needs you. He needs to go forward, so march, draw your sword, do what you're called to do.

Jesus gave us one instruction, and that is to come and follow him. There are some people here tonight who had serious issues of following people instead of following Jesus. The Lord brought me here to tell you come. As you surrender everything, I ask him to bring Jesus into your heart and to fill you afresh and renew you with the precious Holy Spirit. Friend, follow Jesus, not man, and watch what he'll do for you. He'll stick with you closer than a brother.

Remember what causes your faith to sink is a broken focus. So we need to stop this stinking thinking and to focus on Jesus. And ladies, focus on Jesus if you looking to God for the right mate in your life.

He brought me here to tell you tonight you're all diamonds and very precious to the Lord. Don't you settle for second-best.

The Lord reserves his best for his people. I'm going to pray over you: "Dear gracious heavenly Father, you told me to pray over all the beautiful ladies out there. If you're believing God for a mate, tonight is your night. He's going to break the nail off you, He's going to place you on the heart of the right person, the one he has designed for you, your colleague, and your family." We need you to receive that. And don't worry. Focus on Jesus, worship him, and read his Word.

Worship, dance, and smile because your best days are ahead. You are now in your next chapter. You are now in your season of acceleration, and the Lord is going to do so much so fast in your life, friend, if you'll be obedient, if you'll follow Jesus and not follow me. Wow, what a great word. Remember it's more than you know.

I release the spirit of grace to all of you. I release the impartation of faith to walk this through. I'm here to tell you that you're more than good enough to handle this. You deserve to have that kingdom marriage that you're dreaming of. Just receive it, walk forward, take the hand of Jesus, and trust him.

There's no place I'd rather be than in the arms of Jesus. Sometimes you have to be with Jesus for a little while. Then he'll bring in the right mate for you and the right friends. Just trust him. Trust him with everything in you because Jesus is the best friend you could ever know. So first and foremost, you need to rededicate your relationship with Jesus. Let's do that tonight. Let's rededicate our covenants to Jesus. Let's take his hand. Let's trust the Lord, and let's sail on.

And to you, I address that you're releasing the right people you want in your life now and removing all the toxic people you do not want in your life now. And I thank you, heavenly Father, for allowing me and showing me how to pull them into my peace and not allow them to toxify my life. See that's what the Lord wants for all of us. He wants us to pull these people into our peace to get them saved. He'll deliver. We are equipped and trained to go forward, but he does not want you and I to allow them to toxify us. You have the right to say no when no means no, and you have the right to say yes when yes means yes. So friend, tonight's your night to surrender that worry completely to your heavenly Father and trust him with everything in you.

I see a radiating light tonight. You're so precious, Sister Crystal and Pat. You guys are so beautiful. The Lord loves you so much, and he's longing to radiate through you.

Go back and read the book of Peter. Remember that Peter is a risk taker, and yes, he had a temper. He kind of reminds me a little bit of me because I get so frustrated. My temper sometimes takes over, and I have to stop it. Go for a walk, and talk to Daddy. I ask, "Daddy, help me with my temper. Break that stubbornness off them in name of Jesus."

Peter also was a water-walker. As I mentioned previously, when he saw Jesus walking on the water, he went for it too. The Lord wants you all to say, "I'm going for it," in Jesus's name because I want to get people saved. I want to get people set free. I want to get these drug addicts into being saved, delivered, and set free. That's what it's all about when you start walking on water. I'm walking in the room called faith. It's going to feel funny because it's not normal. But the more you read the Bible, the more you pray. and the more you go to church, faith is going to start flowing. The Lord becomes most of your life.

When you're walking in the spiritual realm and not in the flesh, it brings in all kinds of chaos.

Nine teenagers were saved at our first family night
revival in Canonsburg, Pennsylvania.

National Day of Prayer in Washington DC, 2020.

My paternal grandmother, Greta Uldrich-
Tichnell, was my dearest mentor.

My support group!

Musician Joe Cota from Dallas, Texas.

Our first mission trip to Brazil.